The Greening

The Story of Nazarene Compassionate Ministries

The Greening

The Story of
Nazarene Compassionate Ministries

by

R. Franklin Cook
and
Steve Weber

Nazarene Publishing House
Kansas City, Missouri

DEDICATED

to
the volunteers
who have been making
it happen all along

Contents

About the Title

Imagine a desert, brown and barren, stretching as far as the eye can see. Science tells us there is life in the desert—rodents, lizards, animals, cacti, snakes, flowers. The mountains are stark and imposing. The desert appears empty of useful product. Yet in most cases the soil possesses ample nutrients to be fertile.

The greening of the desert can result from an application of water. Out of brown barrenness can erupt a fertile greening.

The greening brings
—lush abundance where there was emptiness
—edible food where there was hunger and starvation
—healing where there existed disease and illness
—new life where death pervaded
—knowledge to minds where there was an uncomprehending stare

The greening reminds us of "streams in the desert" (Isa. 35:6). Jesus explained compassionate ministry as "a cup of cold water" (Matt. 10:42). It is the water that can be poured on a parched land.

Jesus is the eternal Water. With Him there is no further thirst. The compassionate ministry of "cold water" is done in the name of Christ.

Foreword

Nazarene missionary work has always been compassionate. The earliest missionaries of the denomination gave attention to mental and physical wants as well as the spiritual needs of the world. Hospitals, clinics, dispensaries, and schools have occupied budget and personnel of World Mission from the very beginning.

Recently, however, Compassionate Ministries has taken on a more formal structure. A Hunger and Disaster Fund was established to assist with the human need in the wake of destructive storms and human tragedy. Nazarenes responded generously and showed their concern in such a great way that the fund was carried on.

In the early 1980s the media graphically brought to our attention the tragic news of starvation, disease, nakedness, earthquakes, and so on all around the world. Nazarenes declared, "We want to do something!" In order to help meet the crying needs of the world and to care properly for the overwhelming response of Nazarenes everywhere, it was proposed to the Board of General Superintendents that a coordinator of Compassionate Ministries be employed to look after this growing work. Steve Weber, missionary to Haiti, was secured. Funds are sent in voluntarily from individuals, churches, districts, college campuses, and some charitable foundations.

In order to take nothing from the funds for evangelism of both home and world missions through the General Budget, an amount not to exceed 15 percent of the Hunger and Disaster Fund was authorized for use to pay salaries and overhead. Readers will note that this is an extremely low figure.

This book, so ably authored by Franklin Cook and Steve Weber, describes both the spirit and the programs that now function within Compassionate Ministries, a significant part of the World Mission Division. It is a thrilling and moving story.

—L. GUY NEES
Director, World Mission Division

Preface

Joint authorship is a strange creature.

First, the authors must agree on a basic philosophy and approach. We have debated several issues described in this book, but find ourselves on the same wave length.

Second, the authors should spend time together to stay "in tune." We have done that in San Diego; in Kansas City; in Miami; in Prescott, Ariz.; and courtesy of AT & T.

Third, readers always wonder "who wrote what part." Don't try! In a sense we both wrote everything. Therefore, each of us will share the compliments and accept the blame!

Finally, the authors thank you, the readers, for reading and for being a part of the picture of compassion.

Acknowledgments

At the risk of overlooking so many who resourced this book, we are compelled to acknowledge the following:

Rodney Adkins—Compassionate Ministries
Randy and Lorie Beckum—Long Beach
Paul Benefiel—Los Angeles
Peter Burkhart—Philippines
Roy Copelin—Philippines
Stephen Doerr—Zambia
Dr. Glenn Fell—Ciskei
Fred Huff—Fiji
Joaquim A. Lima—Brazil
Dr. J. V. Morsch—Central Florida
Dr. Carlos Helmar Juaréz Moya—Guatemala
Mrs. Carolyn Myatt—India
Robert Prescott—Compassionate Ministries
Nathan Price—Central Florida
Hubert Rabon—NTS and staff
Margi Scott—Portugal
Stanley Storey—El Salvador

And to everyone else, thank you.

"The Nazarene Compassionate Ministries program has been thrust upon us by the conscience of the church."

—L. Guy Nees

In the Beginning

"I'm so happy that the Church of the Nazarene is starting Compassionate Ministries." This statement has been heard many times since the creation of the office of coordinator of Nazarene Compassionate Ministries in June 1984. Nothing could be farther from reality. The compassionate outreach of the church has been part of its creed and very soul much before Pilot Point. This book is at least a beginning of the attempt to remind many of us where we came from as a church. These concerns and ministries made the people called Nazarenes effective in changing their world for Jesus. For many new Nazarenes, this will all be new information. It can help rekindle the early spirit of compassionate outreach and concern for those who are less fortunate than ourselves and in desperate need to hear, "Jesus loves you," in action as well as word.

Perhaps the statement by so many that they are delighted with the "beginning" of Nazarene Compassionate Ministries is their way of saying they are pleased to see the denomination highlight these ministries. No doubt there has been a concern that overemphasizing these exciting ministries might lead to neglect or deemphasis on the primary focus of missions: evangelism. In the beginning let us make one thing clear. The Nazarene Compassionate Ministries effort is based on the solid biblical foundation that mandates the involvement of holiness people in ministry to the "poor of the land." We have done, and will always do, these types of ministries because Jesus told us to do these things. Not to do them is to not have the love of Jesus in us. They are part of evangelism; they result in evangelism. The church is built as a result.

The old battle between the social gospel and evangelism must be laid to rest. Nazarenes are involved in these ministries because they are humanitarian and concerned with social issues. We involve ourselves in these ministries because we must reach out and help those who are less fortunate than ourselves. But here is the big plus that makes the difference: *We reach out in the name of Jesus.* We give the cup of cold water *in the name of Jesus.* Our acts of compassion are part of evangelism. Men are not chopped into pieces called souls, bodies, and minds. Each is part of a whole that has been created in the image of God. We do acts of compassion in the attempt to lead men to complete restoration in the image of God. This means freedom from sin and the opportunity to experience the fullness of life and wholeness that comes only through knowing the saving power of Jesus Christ.

But how does Nazarene Compassionate Ministries determine where to begin? There are literally billions of people in need around the globe. How are priorities determined? How are resources allocated and distributed? How are the limited resources applied to the unlimited needs?

The primary consideration is the location of the established Church of the Nazarene. It is much more effective to minister relief where there are already established churches. In these cases, it is the normal church structure (pastors, church administrators, missionaries) that determines the needs, the types of ministry, and the extent of response.

Disaster and tragedy often occur where there is no established Church of the Nazarene. Or perhaps the church is new or small. To guide in these situations a list of priorities has been established by the Nazarene Hunger and Disaster Relief Fund Committee:

14

First: Nazarenes in acute need (disaster or poverty that places the lives and existence of Nazarenes in danger).

Second: The poorest of the poor. This group is defined as those people who earn the equivalent of under $250 U.S. per year. There are approximately 800 million such people living in the world today. It is quite clear that Nazarene Compassionate Ministries cannot respond to all of these people. But as opportunity presents itself, such as in Ethiopia, Sudan, Bangladesh, Haiti, and other areas comprising the poorest of the poor, Nazarene Compassionate Ministries does all that is possible to minister to these desperate people in the midst of their extreme poverty.

Third: Refugees. There are approximately 16 million people of our world who can never go home. They have lost their home or have been forced to leave their home. They are displaced, alone, and in search of help, comfort, and aid. They are prime candidates for ministry in Jesus' name. Nazarene Compassionate Ministries is seeking to make that ministry the reality of the love of Jesus Christ through acts of compassion.

Fourth: The relative poor of developed nations such as the United States and similar countries. It is obvious that there are few if any people living in the United States who earn under $250 per year. Yet there are millions in the United States who exist on under $4,000 per year. These are the jobless, the new arrivals, the homeless. These are the poor who live in desperate situations of real poverty. To these people we must offer our concern.

The various responses to these categories of needy people are discussed and explained in the chapters to follow. These are exciting stories of sacrifice, unbelievable suffering, and profound pain. One cannot read the following pages without feeling a twinge of guilt, for most readers of this book live in relative wealth. But guilt is not the purpose of these pages. The purpose is to share the growing and amazing accounts of Nazarenes ministering around our world to people in need. A deep sense of gratefulness should quickly replace that guilt twinge. We are a part of a great body of believers that cares for others and is daily showing concern and Christlike compassion.

What are the whos, whats, and hows of Nazarene Compassionate Ministries? The office of Nazarene Compassionate Ministries is located in Kansas City and is part of the World Mission Division.

This office is charged with the coordination of the various Compassionate Ministries activities of the church around the world. The various types of ministries defined as compassionate ministries are: disaster relief, feeding programs, agmissions, self-help, medical missions, vocational training, formal and nonformal education, and refugee assistance.

But who actually performs these ministries? That is the untold story of Nazarene Compassionate Ministries. There are hundreds of Nazarene missionaries, pastors, and church leaders who may or may not be officially listed as "compassionate" on the rolls of headquarters personnel files. These are those who are confronted by unbelievable need and simply do the obvious: They react like Jesus would react. They cry, they suffer, they respond with whatever resources they can muster to make the hurting stop. These are the doctors, nurses, agricultural specialists, farmers-turned-preachers, and a host of volunteers with specialized training that often means the difference between life and death.

A question that is often asked: "How many missionaries are involved in Compassionate Ministries?" The question doesn't have any one answer. The volcano erupts, and the Bible school director becomes the disaster relief coordinator for the area. The earthquake strikes Mexico City, and the district superintendent, Advisory Board, and members from the local Nazarene seminary all become willing participants in the Disaster Relief Committee. Between 30 percent and 40 percent of all Nazarene missionaries are involved in some type of Compassionate Ministries. Over 100 are devoting full time in these ministries. The rest are willing volunteers filling the gap in addition to church planting, teaching in Bible schools, evangelism, or administration.

A growing list of NIVS (Nazarenes In Volunteer Service) are ministering in these areas of need. Of course, the national church is deeply involved. One begins to see a picture of a very large and effective "delivery system of mercy" through the Nazarene structure. Most of this "compassionate corps" are simply "being Jesus" to people in desperate need. Few seek, but all deserve, praise for the ministry of compassion they are carrying out through the Church of the Nazarene.

Compassionate ministry has nothing at all to do with geography, but everything to do with bridging the gaps that separate the believing Christian from a world in need. Many times that separation is caused by oceans, mountains, or language and distance. But many other times that separation is caused by color of skin, economic status, or the location of one's home and church in relation to the poor of our own communities. May God help us all to be sensitive to the needs we should see all around us. If we respond with Christ's love in positive acts of compassion to these needs, desperate people can find peace and fulfillment and become all that God intends.

"To look into the eyes of a starving child is to look into the eyes of a dying soul."
                                    —Richard Schubert

1

Silent Babies

The wind was hot and searing as it cut across the plains of northeast Africa. It dried the skin and burned the eye. Relentlessly it whipped through mountains and valleys, broadening across the expanse of what were once fertile fields, picking up bits of dust and straw and carrying them out to the Arabian Sea.

Leonard Mbuze had been born to raise crops. His father, his father's father, and all the known generations before him had worked the land. There had been times of dryness before, but this time was possibly the worst of all. Certainly it was the worst in Leonard's memory.

Mbuze peered across the dying sprouts of what was to have been a life-giving crop. His gaze drifted toward the horizon. Two or three white puffs of clouds drifted aimlessly from west to east. It was monsoon season. The skies should be leaden with moisture; instead they were a gray-blue cast, burning with heat, dryness, and relentless wind. This was the third year. The famine would continue, and added thousands would starve.

Ponds, where cattle and birds came to drink, had long ago dried. The earth had crusted into large, gaping cracks. Lakes had diminished to meager spots of wetness. Rivers were nothing but rock-strewn scars on the landscape. Without the benefit of dams or springs of water, thirst would join hunger in a marriage of death.

Geraldine Scott, a nurse attached to Church World Service, was spending her time with the children in a disaster relief camp near the Mbuze farm. Over 70 percent of the children were below standard height or weight. Relief supplies had arrived, and six small meals were being provided per day, consisting of high protein biscuit, porridge, dried skim milk, soy, pea flour, oil and sugar mixture, and wheat porridge.

But these children were the fortunate few. They had reached the camp. Most of the children had not. Of those reaching the camp, 40 percent had protein energy malnutrition (PEM). Many were extremely dehydrated and required rehydration with Hartman's solution or oral rehydration salts.

The camp was a haven. Yet all the major medical problems aggravated by famine were there: pneumonia; malaria; TB; parasitical, malnutritional, and bacterial diarrhea; and an assortment of diseases associated with vitamin deficiency, such as beriberi, pellagra, and Vita A.

The children were under 24-hour watch, divided into treatment, cleanup and shower, and feeding-sections. Those children unable to eat are either put on IVs, a feeding nasogastric tube, or force-fed with cups or 20-cc syringes. Usually 24-72 hours of such treatment result in an upswing. For those who die, grieving families stoically accept the bodies for burial and death rites. Death is so common that burial is an hourly event. And those in this camp are the fortunate few.

Monsoon is an Arabic term meaning "seasons." In much of the equatorial world, this change of season—the monsoon—spells life or death. When the rain comes, there is feasting and celebration. When the rain fails, there is hunger and famine. When climatic conditions prevent the monsoon

20

from arriving for several consecutive years, death and disaster are the result. And that has been the condition along the 22 nations in the "famine belt" of Africa.

Even with the media blitz, the million-selling "Africa Live Aid" record, and the enormous worldwide response to this human disaster, in 1985 the United Nations Food and Agricultural Surveys estimated food shortfalls at these levels:

	Thousands of Tons
Angola	217
Botswana	52
Burkina Faso	110
Burundi	67
Cape Verde	61
Chad	225
Ethiopia	1,200
Guinea	64
Kenya	310
Lesotho	70
Morocco	120
Mozambique	575
Niger	350
Rwanda	69
Somalia	75
Tanzania	236
Zimbabwe	140

These amounts, it is estimated, were needed simply to keep the Mbuze family and entire populations from starving.

Nazarene Compassionate Ministries (NCM) has been part of the rapid response, joining hands with other agencies where needed, and finding ways of reaching areas out of reach of other agencies. A primary source of money has been the Hunger and Disaster Fund, to which Nazarenes have been giving with increasing frequency.

Relief agencies must generate overhead and operational

expenses out of income received. These amounts range from 19 percent to 63 percent of total monies collected. NCM has operated on 15 percent overhead, with 100 percent of all *designated* monies going to their purpose.

THE ADKINS FACTOR

Rodney Adkins has been a volunteer most actively involved in food distribution and famine relief. Adkins, a Nazarene layman, had owned and operated a chain of grocery stores in West Virginia. Having been successful in the food industry, he was financially able to offer himself several years ago to the general church for volunteer service. He felt God was calling him into this type of ministry.

But the general church did not know where or how to use a person with Rodney Adkins' skills. That is, until an office of Compassionate Ministries was established with a full-time coordinator. It was an office immediately confronted with monsoon failure—and a massive human tragedy in Africa. Adkins, a food distrubtion expert; NCM, with a mandate and a fund to administer; an African famine of Herculean proportions—all converged at about the same time in what must be God's timing.

EXAMPLES OF RESPONSE

Ethiopia

It was nightfall in Shashemene, Ethiopia. The only hotel in the village had seen better days. Its red-tiled roof and white-columned porch had a veneer of dust and a generous sprinkling of cobwebs.

Rodney Adkins and Harmon Schmelzenbach II, pioneer missionary to Kenya, had checked in for the night. They were on a trip to interior Ethiopia, surveying the famine disaster and establishing contacts for Nazarene response.

Adkins and Schmelzenbach noticed two dozen vultures roosting on the roof, casting glances at these two visitors. Occasionally a group of the vultures would rise and circle the hotel before settling back to roost again. The team of two, traveling by Land Rover, had seen death and vultures all day. No doubt these birds were pleased at the feasting prospects presented by two living people.

All day Adkins and Schmelzenbach had traveled hard out of the capital city of Addis Ababa, eventually dropping off the inland plateau and following a chain of lakes down the Rift Valley. The land was dry with no standing crops right up to the lake's edge. Connecting rivers between lakes, usually broad and full, were dry.

Struggling to cope with the devastation were volunteers serving with a number of relief agencies. In one case, two Europeans and one African Catholic sister were attempting to feed several thousand starving who pressed around one camp. Medical reports were kept on each family, and dry food for one week was given to each family unit. It was obvious that many would not live.

In Ethiopia, Nazarenes have cooperated with the Christian Relief and Development Association (CRDA), the agency approved by the government for relief work.

In a letter written days after this first visit, Harmon Schmelzenbach reflects:

> There are simply no words adequate to describe the scene in those camps. Thousands of people, most of them sitting in total silence, even the babies. At a glance you can tell those who will live and those who will not. You can literally see when the light has gone in their eyes and hope has died. It is an awesome experience. I found it almost impossible to take a picture or two for our church publications.

Two expatriate Irish nurses were running a camp near Sodo. They were feeding 2,000 people daily. In addition, distribution of maize, dry milk, sorghum, and cooking oil was made to the extent it was available. The camp (typical of such camps) consisted of a windmill water well, nurses' station, cooking shed, two holding sheds, and two medical and feeding sheds. This well-organized camp, falling ever further behind, was turning 2,000 starving people away *daily* for lack of food and supplies.

Rodney Adkins writes: "Bir Bir seems to be among the worst drought-stricken areas in the south of Ethiopia. It looks as if the people are constantly ploughing different areas of their land in anticipation of rain, but none seems to have fallen in over a year."

Ethiopia is only one nation affected by the drought and famine.

Kenya

In Nairobi, Kenya, Leo Mpoke, a local Kenyan Nazarene, has been appointed coordinator for developmental ministries, East Africa. He works with Harmon Schmelzanbach II on the refugee problem created in southern Sudan and other areas caused by the killer drought.

Mr. Mpoke is a graduate of Spring Arbor College in Michigan and is a preacher's son. His availability and expertise has been a godsend for the church. He has spent hundreds of hours shuttling from office to office, securing permits and permissions, standing in lines to catch overcrowded airplanes, and caring for a multitude of necessary details.

Money sent by Nazarenes designated for Kenya has supported six large camps housing several thousand children. These camps are administered by the Africa Inland Mission and sit near Lake Rudolf.

Money buys not only food but medical supplies. In one case in Kenya, for example, funds purchased several small, kerosene-burning refrigerators for remote clinics where no electricity is available. Snakebite serum, penicillin, and other medical supplies requiring refrigeration are preserved.

Drilling equipment to assist in water acquisition has also been funded in cooperation with other mission agencies. Only dependable water supplies can erase the panic exodus from some areas.

And Clothes Too!

The booking number was NY HOW 7290080. One 40-foot container, marked "Clothing," contained 364 cartons of used clothing, each containing 100 pounds. Each carton, labeled either "Men," "Women," or "Children," was 51 cubic feet in size. The total net weight of the shipment was 36,560 pounds.

The Kansas City district NWMS had been asked to fill a semitrailer with used clothing in six weeks. Those in charge said, "We'll do it," although later some admitted they silently added, "At least we'll try."

All 72 churches of the district participated. Each church was given empty cartons. Each church brought filled cartons on the scheduled day to Mid-America Nazarene College, where it was loaded onto the truck. The churches generated 45,000 pounds of clothing, more than enough to fill the container.

Now the container was aboard the *American Argo,* sailing from New Orleans on April 29 and arriving in Maputo, capital of Mozambique, on May 24. From there the clothing was distributed through a network of Nazarene churches to thousands who had literally run out of garments.

Red Tape

Work within a disaster context still requires working through red tape. In the case of Mozambique, the government, through Minister of Justice Job Mabanani Chambal, gave permission to do feeding and medical response programs.

In Mozambique, Nazarenes have had a church presence for years and built up a strong network of contacts. Rev. Salomao Macie, district superintendent of the Maputo District, has supervised the food distribution programs. Rev. Macie also serves as president of the Christian Council of Churches in Mozambique, a nongovernmental private organization actively involved in liaison with the government and food distribution nationwide.

Because many countries in this area are politically sensitive, all those actively involved have cultivated contacts and worked cooperatively with governmental authorities. The importation of food, clothing, and medical supplies requires legal permission as well as a trustworthy system of distribution.

In most cases, Nazarenes have dealt with the heads of cabinet offices or major governmental agencies designated to supervise relief and developmental projects. Rodney Adkins has developed high skill at this.

The Venda Project

The Church of the Nazarene provided substantial money to the Venda District in southern Africa to assist in a famine amid severe drought. By estimate 160 families representing 600 people were given life out of certain death because of Hunger and Disaster Fund allocations.

Pastor Mavhetha of the local Folovhodwe church was responsible for distribution of the "mealie meals." On one occasion he gathered all the designated needy families in his local church for a short service. Many had never been in church before.

A letter from the headman (mayor) in this area to the church expresses thanks.

Dear Sir:

I as the headman of Folovhodwe location feel honoured, happy, and thank the power of Glory who sees the suffering of this people—about the drought, who send this people some bags of mealies. Little gift brings happiness both to the donor and the recipient (Matt. 7:7-11). The Church of the Nazarene is a small building, but it does a lot. Long live—long live the organizers.

Yours faithfully,
Headman P. T. Nefolovhodwl

Immediate disaster and food relief is a process that is ongoing worldwide. For example, the church is sending tons of powdered milk to several areas of the world. In some cases excess food from one part of the world is being sent to a needy area.

All these efforts are coordinated through NCM. The regional directors are active participants in the process. In the case of the African disaster, Regional Director Dr. Richard Zanner has not only supported but given hands-on site work in several projects.

FEEDING IS NOT ENOUGH

Ultimately, to feed alone is not enough. One of the most important aspects of dealing with famine is through developmental projects and through what has come to be known as "agmissions."

As the name suggests, agmissions is the application of agricultural technology to a mission need. This is expressed through NCM in many ways (which will be explained in a later chapter) such as seed and implement distribution. Seed commodities recently distributed are peanuts, seed corn, cow peas, red beans, tomato, pumpkin, onion, cabbage, lettuce, and squash. Implements such as plows, hoes, shovels, and rakes are included.

FINALLY . . .

In the African famine most babies die at night. In extreme malnutrition, babies are too weak to eat, to drink, or to cry. They remain silent and starving. At night, they are too weak to shiver—and thus, even in relatively mild climates, they die of the cold. There are thousands of silent babies. The church is rescuing a few—in the name of Christ.

"Don't domesticate compassion."   —Paul Rees

"The first service of a Holy Ghost-baptized church is to the
poor."   —Phineas F. Bresee

2

Full Circle

ENGAGEMENT

It is difficult to overstate the zeal and fervor of early
holiness leaders. They roared themes of righteousness and
warned against social evils. Generally they were an activist
lot, not afraid to speak boldly, take stands on controversial
issues, and step out recklessly in action. In a word, they were
engaged with the world.

In the early 1900s issues included liquor, support for
women's suffrage (it is worth noting that Nazarenes have
always ordained female elders), and rescuing the poor and
downtrodden victims of the industrial revolution in American cities.

By the time of the 1908 merger in Pilot Point, Tex., the
newly formed Church of the Nazarene was sponsoring or
supporting rescue homes for fallen women, orphanages (usually adjacent to the rescue homes), and rescue missions in the
cities. (Note appendix for a listing.) Other specific concerns
included prison ministries, medical care, and ministries to

immigrants, such as Mexican rail workers in Los Angeles, Japanese and Chinese arrivals on the West Coast, and native Americans on reservations.

Dr. Timothy L. Smith, author of *Called unto Holiness,* states, "The chief aim of the church was to preach holiness to the poor . . . the first *Manual* announced the church's determination to win the lost through the agency of city missions, evangelistic services, house-to-house visitation, caring for the poor, comforting the dying" (113-14).

Bresee's church in Los Angeles set apart deaconesses for Christian service. Their assignment was to distribute clothing to the poor and medical assistance to the ill.

In the East, William Howard Hoople and Charles BeVier launched their work in 1894 in a Brooklyn saloon. A. B. Riggs in 1904 commended the New England Holiness Association for their "devotion . . . to rescue work and relief for the poor."

J. O. McClurkan's Pentecostal Mission in Nashville, which did not merge with Nazarenes until 1915, was early on involved in mission and rescue home work. They affiliated with the Door of Hope Mission and sponsored the Pentecostal Mission Training Home for Girls.

Phoebe Palmer, in her book *The Promise of the Father,* declared, "Pentecost laid the axe at the root of social injustice."

Seth Cook Rees wrote in 1905 a book titled *Miracles in the Slums.* Among many incidents, he recalls sponsoring a converted prostitute in opening a rescue home in New York City, which consisted of a two-room apartment equipped with straw mats and crates for furniture.

In middle America the well-known Rest Cottage in Pilot Point was founded in 1903. Many people supported the effort faithfully. For example, the 1912 Kansas District Assembly pledged $546 in support of the home for wayward girls. This social ministry continued until 1972, during which over 4,500 girls were assisted.

A committee of the Second General Assembly (1911) on rescue work, chaired by J. T. Upchurch, states the social evil of white slavery in vivid terms:

> Young American girls are shipped to China, Japan, India, and other countries, where they are sold to men of wealth for the vilest purposes . . . We are informed that when a man of wealth tires of one of our little American girls, he either sends her to a brothel or has her head cut off (*Journal of Second General Assembly,* 1911, 43-44).

The report continues by condemning the importation of oriental girls into America:

> Possibly the most horrible thought in connection with this international traffic in human souls is of a Christian (?) America in receiving little girls from other countries to be disposed of through the shambles of shame in the scarlet districts of our great cities, where the most terrible atrocities are heaped upon them, the horrors of which are sufficient to pale the cheeks of darkness (Ibid., 44).

J. T. Upchurch founded the Berachah Home in Arlington, Tex., for "the redemption and protection of erring girls." The home operated from 1903 to 1942, at which time it closed after the general church declined to assume direct supervision.

Perhaps the most ambitious social institution the church was involved with in the United States was the Samaritan Hospital in Nampa, Idaho, founded in 1920 by Dr. Thomas E. Mangum. This hospital, called The Nazarene Missionary Sanitarium and Institute, serviced several generations of missionaries. Many missionary nurses took specialized training at the school of nursing, which graduated its first class in 1931. By the mid 1950s, the entire visionary venture was closed, with the nurses' residence and unfinished hospital wing purchased and converted to other uses by Northwest Nazarene College.

DISENGAGEMENT

Social concern of the general church for compassionate ministry reached its zenith at the 1919 General Assembly. Five General Assembly committees were related to social welfare work. District boards of social welfare were strongly encouraged and a five-member Orphange Board was elected. There were continuing committees on rescue work and city missions.

The year 1923 seems to have been a watershed in disengaging from many of these activities. In that year many previously semiautonomous committees were consolidated into a General Board, a basic structure which still exists. By 1928 only three of the five General Assembly committees concerned with social welfare remained (Social Welfare and Orphanage, Deaconess, and State of the Church and Public Morals). In 1932 these three were lumped under one committee, and in 1948 this committee became simply the State of the Church and Public Morals.

Why the dramatic shift? Dr. J. Fred Parker, in his excellent analysis in an article titled "Those Early Nazarenes Cared," suggests four reasons:

1. The financial squeeze made support of many institutions burdensome. (It is important to remember the Great Depression occurred during this time, which had worldwide reverberations and resulted in a dramatic retrenchment in foreign missions.)

2. There was a mild revolt, or pendulum swing, against institutions as adjuncts of the church, whose central mission was seen as saving souls. In an address to the 1923 General Assembly the general superintendents said, "Every effort should be made to keep down institutionalism."

3. Underlying many attitudes was a pervasive feeling that somehow social action meant "social gospel," and social gospel was equated with theological liberalism and biblical higher criticism. It is helpful to note that in those days socialism was a political philosophy influencing many American and European universities.

4. There was a change in editorship of the *Herald of Holiness*, the official organ of the denomination. Many columns of space had been devoted, under the editorship of B. F. Haynes, an outspoken activist, to the social evils of the day. Haynes minced no words in his editorials.

With the arrival of Dr. J. B. Chapman as editor, there was a perceptible shift in the content of the magazine toward education, missions (meaning "foreign missions"), and church growth. It is difficult to say whether these were by design, by temperament of the editor, or simply a reflection of changing social attitudes in the church.

In foreign missions, compassionate ministry was standard practice. Health care, education, printing, feeding the hungry, even agricultural training were accepted as the norm. Back home, these activities were questioned as being out of the purview of an evangelistic church.

General superintendents, even into the 1960s and 1970s, warned that institutions would sap the spiritual vitality of the church. One general superintendent advised that the church had no business sponsoring retirement high-rise projects or using outside money to fund special ministries.

Meanwhile, during this period of disengagement, a visionary corps of Nazarenes struggled on in the urban centers of North America, contending with all the old-new problems of alcohol, drug dependency, homelessness, unemployment, immigrants, race relations and civil rights, food and clothing distribution, and preventative and curative health care.

The philosophical debate continued in an effort to discover the most effective means to win people to Christ and at the same time minister to the whole man in His name.

REENGAGEMENT

The use of this term is dangerous. Some will claim the church never disengaged. Others will claim the church is still disengaged. Yet others will debate just when and how there was a reengagement.

As stated earlier, outstanding examples of engagement can be cited all over the nation, even during what these authors have defined as disengagement. True, the officially sponsored rescue homes, hospitals, orphanages, and homes had all disappeared. A few city missions, notably the Kansas City Rescue Mission, remained, largely because of the dedication of faithful financial contributors.

In a 1982 survey, the Department of Church Extension discovered over 2,000 local Nazarene churches doing some type of compassionate ministry. There were outstanding examples of ministry, such as: the Community of Hope of Dr. Tom Nees in Washington, D.C.; New World Ministries, founded by Gilbert Leigh in Chicago; Christian Counseling Services, inspired by the vision of Dr. William Slonecker in Nashville and supported by the Tennessee District; the Lamb's ministry in New York City, heavily supported by the New York District and the general church; and others too numerous to mention.

Of course, compassionate ministry around the world never abated.

However, for purposes of this book, we identify reengagement to mean the 1984 creation of an office of Compassionate Ministries with a full-time international coordinator and based at International Headquarters in Kansas City. This office answers to a governing committee consisting of the directors of the Divisions of World Mission and of Church Growth, the vice-chairman of the Board of General Superintendents, and the general secretary of the denomination. Any project over $25,000 must be approved by this group.

Much of this book relates the exciting story of reengagement, as the Church of the Nazarene explores the meaning of its roots, its theology, and its mission extending into the 21st century.

(Note the Appendix for a listing of social compassion institutions in North America sponsored officially and unofficially but whose names appear in official church records.)

"I do not see the Wounded Man. I became the wounded man."
                                                    —Walt Whitman

"Good works are not random options of the gospel."
                                                    —John L. Peters

3

Why?

The Church of the Nazarene is heavily engaged in compassionate ministries around the world. It is time to look at why we do these types of ministries. This chapter does not seek to be exhaustive (and we hope not exhausting!), but rather act as a thought-provoker. The rationale behind our ministries is important and should be firmly based in God's directives as found in His Word.

Jesus reminds us there have always been poor people and always will be. Some people conclude we should simply feed the poor and accept the status quo. The question is, "What is God's perfect plan?"

Christians who have been blessed with material possessions have a tremendous responsibility to account for all God has given. Other benefits of our life-style for so many of us include such things as literacy, curative health facilities which are literally around the corner, sufficient pure water, and other natural resources to sustain life in a very comfortable manner.

This raises certain questions, such as responsible consumption patterns for Christians. In other words, how much can we spend upon ourselves, when we live and work in a world which suffers from a tremendously unjust system of distribution? On the one hand, we have more than sufficient resources to provide for the essentials of life: food, clothing, shelter, health facilities, and so on. On the other hand, we are becoming increasingly aware of the billions of people on this planet who do not have many of these things all of us would define as "necessities." Approaching God's Word, then, with this unjust system of distribution in mind, we are confronted with some troubling choices that are not easy to make and yet that must be made. Such scriptures as Matthew chapter 25 talk about God's judgment upon those with material possession who did not share them with those in need. What then is defined as "share" or as "need"?

God had a type of economy in mind. It is an economy that does not allow us to live as if material questions have nothing to do with spiritual values. It is clear from Scripture God never intended for us to live as if we could ignore the poverty and social evils surrounding us. As evangelicals, we preach, teach, and react strongly against individual sins but often remain uninterested in social evils.

God has a very special place in His heart for the poor of our world (Psalm 146; 1 Sam. 2:1-10). The Christian needs to understand that starvation, poverty, and many of the evils of our day are a direct result of the breakdown of the equitable distribution of resources of our world. Sin has caused our world to be selfish and self-centered. God's Word reminds us it is the Church's responsibility to care and minister to the victims of this misallocation of His resources (victims such as widows, orphans, and refugees). The Old Testament gives 210 references that speak of the responsibility of God's people to the victims of material poverty. Do we need additional prodding?

The New Testament is even more clear. In fact, we find Jesus identifying with the poor and telling us of His anointing to preach to them. Our problem is this: The New Testament clearly teaches that excess consumption is sin. Jesus has reminded us to pay close attention to the needs of the poor and to not be overly anxious about material possessions. We are told to denounce any system of exploitation of the poor and to minister to the victims of these unjust human systems.

The Early Church soon realized that a relief program for the poor must be instituted (Acts 6:1). While there are no universal directives that would tell us all to sell the farm and give the money to the poor, we are constantly reminded of our need to be actively involved in ministering to the needs of those who are in economic need. We have no final law in the church as to the precise form our relief work should take. We do have sufficient mandates to tell us that we must develop a strategy to avoid the extremes of wealth and poverty within the church (2 Cor. 8:13-14; 9:13; Rom. 15:25-26). The system our church has developed through Compassionate Ministries is one concrete way in which all can participate in this scriptural admonition. It is hard to justify any type of overindulgence when there are countless millions in our world with literally nothing to eat.

From the New Testament through the middle ages, from John Wesley to Bresee, we in the Nazarene heritage have much tradition that should help us to establish our response to the poor and needy of our world.

John Wesley, in his journal dated May 7, 1741, wrote clearly about feeding the hungry, clothing the naked, creating job programs for the unemployed, caring for the sick and homeless. Most of these programs Christians in the United States have largely delegated to the government. Wesley was clear in his feelings that the Church is the only viable approach to changing society. Without also taking care of the sin problem, all the welfare programs in the world aren't going to make much difference in our troubled world. But with the message of heart purity, we can minister to the poor of our world and offer them a message of complete hope and wholeness. No other agency can duplicate this.

Dr. Phineas F. Bresee and other early leaders had a great concern for the total person. Dr. Paul Benefiel, church pastor and leader in the Los Angeles area, has said: "They could not, with clear conscience, simply preach to the people, but were moved with compassion to care for the physical needs as well."

Our conclusion is simple. Compassion is at the very heart of the gospel. We don't do these things in place of evangelism, but we do them because of Scripture. The love of Christ within us compels us to become involved (1 John 3:17-18; James 1:27).

So then, why? Because we can see beyond the unfortunate equating of social gospel with a theology of liberalism. We can see beyond a narrow interpretation of evangelism as only saving souls. We can see that holiness suggests a ministry to the whole person, both individually and collectively. In a phrase, compassion (suffering with and motivated to act) is part of Christ's Great Commission to win the world. Compassion is part of Commission.

"I am mute at the world's great sadness." —Paul Rees
"Love must be shared if it is to be shown."
—George Hoffman

4

Emergency!

Disaster! It is just a word in the vocabulary unless you are personally affected. Lulled into a sense of security and self-sufficiency, many people are unable to face the instantaneous change that comes from natural and man-made disasters.

In disasters that capture the Western media's attention, the extent of damage and loss of life is enormous. With the magnitude of such disasters, the amount and duration of response is also enormous. "How can my $10.00 make any difference?" is a not uncommon statement.

It is apparent that the Church of the Nazarene is in no position to take the place of governmental agencies that allocate millions of dollars to meet needs resulting from disaster. There are thousands of para-church and other nongovernmental agencies that appeal for our money and for the most part do a tremendous job of meeting needs.

Why then should the church become involved at all? With so many other agencies doing the job, why don't we just leave disaster response to the professionals?

The reason for our involvement centers around the availability of an effective delivery system. The church is the best and most efficient delivery system available in most disasters. The church is already there. It has a staff of honest, caring people, who are ready to help. There is normally a building. There is always an administrative structure headed by the pastor and key laymen who have various professional and vocational skills that are invaluable in times of emergency. The resources of the church are normally called into action the moment disaster strikes. It is an opportunity to live out the gospel of the love of Jesus.

Can you imagine the cost of duplicating the resources that exist in the church during a time of disaster? Suppose the large disaster agency did not have the church delivery system there to help? To find alternative structures and personnel is time-consuming and often impossible.

In this chapter we present some case studies of the Church of the Nazarene in action during disaster situations. The very beginning of the Nazarene Hunger and Disaster Fund traces its establishment to a massive earthquake in Guatemala. That disaster highlights another key point: In most disasters, the needs of the church to rebuild churches and parsonages are not addressed by any other disaster agency. Many missionaries and church leaders have been eternally grateful to the church for having available the material resources to put the church back on its feet after disaster has struck. (This point may not have quite the impact on readers who live in nations where insurance is available for everything from the family dog to a hung fingernail. If you lived in a country where insurance is either nonexistent or totally beyond your resources to purchase, the impact of disaster would be felt more keenly.)

Mexico City—September 1985

Mexico City is the world's largest metropolitan area, with 18 million living in this geographical basin that was formerly Lake Texcoco. In this dynamic city there are barrios that did not exist 10 years ago, each containing 2 or 3 million people.

Mexico City was already struggling with problems of air pollution (just breathing is said to be the equivalent of smoking two packs of cigarettes a day), 14,000 tons of garbage a day, underemployment of 40 percent, and most of all, jobless peasants streaming into the city at the rate of 1,000 a day. Into this setting roared two gigantic earthquakes. The toll in human life and property was astronomical. The final figures will never be known for sure, but over 10,000 lost their lives, many thousands more were injured, and nearly 1 million people lost their homes. Hundreds of businesses were either immediately destroyed or were later condemned as unsafe.

Of the six Nazarene churches receiving damage, all were repaired with the help of Nazarene Compassionate Ministries and/or Nazarene Work and Witness teams.

Three Nazarene parsonages were destroyed. The office of the Central district superintendent was damaged to the point it had to be demolished and rebuilt, with assistance from NCM. Many additional Nazarene families also lost their homes and have been provided with construction grants through a disaster response committee set up by NCM and funded through the Nazarene Disaster Fund, earmarked especially for Mexico City.

Many Nazarene Mexican medical doctors, lawyers, civil engineers, social workers, and other laymen rushed to assist in this disaster. Four Nazarene churches were used in various aspects of the disaster response. Temporary shelter and feeding of both the displaced persons and rescue workers went on for weeks in some churches. Preventive health care services were provided by Nazarene doctors in these shelters as well.

The Mexico City earthquake response stands as a tribute to Nazarene missions. The Mexican church did the major portion of the disaster response without outside assistance.

When the enormity of the need became apparent, NCM funding was provided, as well as five airplane loads of relief supplies. Dozens of trained Mexican professionals, Nazarene laymen giving of themselves in ministry, is the heart of the story. Our churches were full as the city looked to Christians for comfort in their time of sorrow and confusion.

The end of the story is unknown. The cleanup and rebuilding continues. Lives saved, comfort offered, and decisions made for eternity can only be known by God. But the church was there and responded when needed. It opened its doors to the poor and needy, and it expressed the love of Jesus in the lives of those in need.

Fiji—1985

The world's media cover major disasters but give only a couple of inches of coverage to minor ones. To those directly affected, *any* disaster is major.

In some cases, NCM responds when needed where there is no church presence. In these situations there is a direct spiritual reason for response.

Such was the case in Fiji in early 1985 when a typhoon destroyed much of that beautiful little island. There were no Nazarenes in Fiji; the church isn't there—yet. What better way to introduce our church than through a disaster response team and relief responses? In this case it was missionary Fred Huff. At the time he was a missionary serving in New Zealand, whose ministry was primarily with Polynesian peoples. He was very much aware of the tragedy that struck their neighbors to the north. With one telephone call to the office of Compassionate Ministries, and coordination with the regional office, Fred was sent to Fiji to do a needs assessment survey. What could we do to help? Here is what resulted:

1. Cash was given for food and shelter relief through the Prime Minister's Hurricane Relief Fund.

2. The purchase and donation of shelter materials to the commissioner of the Western Division of the country.

3. Jasper Williams Secondary School was given assistance in the reconstruction of the dining hall and the girl's hostel.

4. Materials were provided for reconstruction of homes of families who lost their homes in the hurricane.

5. Bibles were provided for distribution to families who lost everything they possessed.

6. Reconstruction materials for primary schools assisted in the reconstruction of classrooms.

There is no Church of the Nazarene in Fiji. Not yet. But when those first missionaries set foot on that island, they will have been preceded by acts of love and compassion in the name of Jesus. These acts of concern are not lost to those who have been helped. With limited resources, it is good stewardship to engage in response through the Nazarene delivery system, in the name of Jesus.

Republic of the Philippines—1984

During the six months of 1984 that the office of NCM was in operation (June through December), there were many disasters. Most significant was the series of hurricanes and volcanic eruptions that shook the Philippine Islands.

An excerpt from Roy Copelin's report from one needs assessment survey trip:

"When we approached Estancia we were amazed at the devastation. Mango, banana, and coconut trees were uprooted. They will be without electricity for months as the light poles and telephone poles were on the ground—some fell in one direction and others in another. I have never seen such devastation."

Anyone who has huddled in the corner of their living room watching trees and pieces of housing fly through the air does not need further explanation of the force and power of a typhoon. Man becomes an insignificant survivor in the midst of such fury. The Philippines have largely recovered from these terrible tragedies. "Love kits" were distributed to the displaced people during their time in the temporary shelters. These love kits contained five kilos of rice (approximately 10 pounds), a can of sardines, and a gospel tract in the local language of Bicol.

Many of these displaced people were introduced to the gospel for the very first time. Some were converted. A new Church of the Nazarene was started as a result of these conversions. Rev. Peter Burkhart was the coordinator for much of these relief activities. Burkhart is one of those unofficial Compassionate Ministries missionaries who, in addition to their regular duties, go the extra mile when disaster strikes. To Rev. Burkhart and all the other volunteers who respond during these times of need, the Church of the Nazarene owes a great debt of gratitude. As they show the love of Jesus to these desperate people, they are spreading His love and our love as well.

The Future

As the office of NCM develops, one thing is very clear; there are many volunteers who want to become involved in these responses. These opportunities and needs will be discussed in a later chapter, but in the context of disaster, the tremendous contribution of Nazarene volunteers needs to be recognized. Where disaster strikes and needs are known, thousands of Nazarenes become involved. Through their prayers, donations to the Hunger and Disaster Fund, donation of needed materials, and giving of their time and talents, lives are saved and needs are met.

One man who symbolizes this tremendous dedication and desire to help is Mr. Ken Key. Ken is a layman from Alabama who has made his business, his airplane, and his staff available to NCM whenever needed. He has purchased supplies, secured countless thousands of dollars of donated commodities, and provided airborne delivery of these supplies whenever called upon. Not many people would have the time, the resources, or the patience to work through the tremendous amount of red tape involved in doing disaster response type of work. Mr. Ken Key typifies what is best in volunteers: an attitude of standing ready to do anything, anywhere, at any time, when called upon by his church.

Another example are the businessmen of Arizona Nazarene Lands, Inc., who have committed themselves to needs assessment and a variety of church-planting projects. It is volunteers such as these who make the program work. And it is the love given by Jesus that motivates it all.

To the hungry, "love is credible because it is edible."
—George Hoffman

"There is never enough to go around."   —Paul McCleary

5

A Piece of Bread

There is nothing that typifies Nazarene Compassionate Ministries in the minds of Nazarenes more than feeding programs financed through the Hunger and Disaster Fund. Faces of little Ethiopian children or images of hungry people everywhere receiving a ration of love from Nazarenes around the world who really do love them.

In 1984, 38 percent of all NCM funding was allocated for feeding programs. Few will ever forget those haunting eyes of the silent babies that stared out at us as we watched the evening news on television. To date, the Nazarene feeding response is nearing $1 million in cash grants to provide thousands of tons of food to help save lives in Africa.

But these are the large, well-publicized stories. The electronic and print media constantly bombard us with the latest pictures of haunting eyes. One of the beauties of the NCM system is the undesignated donation. "Send the money where it is most needed." Trust and confidence in a system that does just that: Send the food where it is most needed. Many times these feeding projects received absolutely no publicity. For political reasons, or lack of media exposure, little is said about the suffering or the dying. But the delivery system is there. The church knows where the needs are, even if CBS or NBC or ABC hasn't yet discovered the need.

This chapter attempts to share some of these lesser-known projects. Feeding starving people can be a risky business. What happens when you run out of money and the people are still hungry? Feeding someone for a few days, or a month, and walking away because there are no more resources available is something that needs to be considered before one starts the feeding process. Hunger is one of the most heart-rending tragedies of our time. In the midst of unbelievable wealth and economic growth, millions of people are hungry. Thousands are dying of starvation at this very moment.

Case Study: Florida Feeding Program

Florida is a very nice place to spend the winter months. Many Americans have made this place "retirement heaven." It is a tropical winter wonderland for many vacationers. For many others, Florida represents a hope of a new life—a life where food, clothing, shelter, and education for their children is more than a dream, but can be reality for those who are willing to work and strive.

There are the Haitians, who come in leaky old boats that wouldn't pass a Coast Guard inspection to float across a 50-foot man-made lake. They come by the thousands. Everything they own is on their backs. Most of the Haitians today are going to Suriname, to Venezuela, or to the Dominican Republic to cut sugarcane.

What about these Haitian boat people? Does the Church of the Nazarene have any obligation to them? The answer to that question can be found in a very unique feeding program financed by NCM on the Central Florida Pioneer Haitian District. This pioneer area is the dream of District Superintendent J. V. Morsch, and led by pioneer area leader Nathan

Price. At first these Haitians were only nameless, faceless Black people who could not speak much English but were willing to do anything, to work long hours, in exchange for a livable wage that would become the means to the fulfillment of their dreams of a better life.

The Central Florida District began to minister to these Haitian strangers. A telephone call from Dr. Morsch to the office of NCM was the beginning of the first feeding program. Why were these Haitians hungry? Because the normal temperatures of central Florida had plummeted to below freezing and killed much of the citrus fruit. With the fruit destroyed by frost, there was no work. With no work to be found, there was no money to buy food. With no money to buy food, these people became no different from other hungry people being helped by NCM on the other side of the globe.

As the feeding program began, and contacts were made, it was discovered that many of these Haitian "strangers" were actually Nazarenes who had left their homeland because of economic hardships. They couldn't speak English, but when interviewed through the interpreters they testified to the same saving and sanctifying power that the officials from the Central Florida District Church of the Nazarene had experienced.

As the relationships grew, it was apparent that more than feeding was needed. These people needed jobs. They needed training in how to find jobs. Some needed medical and legal care. All needed a place to worship and praise God. Rev. Nathan Price, pastoring a strong local church, responded to this latter need. He asked to lead the Haitian pioneer area. With full support from the Central Florida District, NCM, and Dr. Bill Sullivan of the Division of Church Growth, Rev. Price has set out to build the Church of the Nazarene among the Haitians in Central Florida. At this writing, nine congregations have been started, and six more are being planted. The first miniassembly of this Haitian District was held in late 1985 in Central Florida. NCM is contributing food, job skills training, income generation projects, and legal aid to these brothers and sisters in the faith. They are anything but "nameless, faceless strangers."

India: Feeding in the Hospital

Another lesser-known feeding project currently being conducted is in India. Under the direction of missionary Mrs. Carolyn Myatt, the patients at the Nazarene hospital in India are fed each day. The feeding of hospital patients may not seem appropriate to running a hospital. But in the developing world, priorities are different than in the developed nations of the West. In most third world hospitals, there is no food. If a person comes to that hospital, the patient must bring his own food. If there are no family members who are able to provide this food, then the patient cannot remain at the hospital, or some other means must be found to feed the person while they recuperate.

Mrs. Myatt requested NCM to help provide the funding for the feeding of these poorest of the poor patients. They have no means of support, and no one to bring them food while they are there. NCM was able, through the Nazarene Hunger and Disaster Fund, to allocate sufficient funds to feed these desperate people. It is a unique feeding program, but necessary in many areas of the developing world.

School Feeding Programs

There is nothing better than a good bowl of soup and a sandwich before going out to play at lunchtime. It is standard fare for millions of youngsters around the developed world. But in many countries, there is no lunch at all. The idea of three meals a day is just an idea. One meager breakfast, consisting of a piece of bread and a cup of water, and the child is sent off to school. If the school has no lunch program, then the child must wait until after sundown, when the evening meal is prepared for the family.

It is not uncommon for a small child to fall asleep during the morning or afternoon lesson at school. Some tumble off of their bench to the hard dirt floor of the church-turned-school building for the week of classes. Can you imagine attempting to learn in such a setting? A hungry stomach, a body even too weak to play! "Jesus may love you, missionary, but your God doesn't even know I exist."

One way to prove the love of Jesus is through the feeding programs of the Nazarene primary and secondary schools found in many lesser-developed countries of our world. The hot lunch in many cases is the only completely balanced and nutritious meal the child will receive. Haiti is an example of a nation that suffers from continuous cycles of crop failures and falls short of adequate food supplies.

In 1976 hot lunch programs were instituted in every Nazarene school in Haiti. Many of these schools are little more than a place to learn how to read and write enough French to be able to qualify for a "real" school in the city. But the 100-plus Nazarene schools are irreplaceable centers of Caravan and Bible study lessons, and a place to receive the hot lunch that just wouldn't be available if there were no Nazarene church in the village.

One might assume the large and well-known agencies would have sufficient resources to help in these feeding programs. Many do. But through the years, these agencies change their objectives, or run out of funds, or must shift their resources to Ethiopia or some other more publicized and needy area. So the problem remains. Thousands of Nazarene children, and others who attend these Nazarene Head Start centers, do so with no hot lunch.

We are working to change that situation. The goal of NCM is to provide a hot meal to every student who attends a Nazarene-sponsored school. In most countries, government or other agencies do this for us. But in Haiti and some places in Africa, we still need help from the family of Nazarenes who want to prove the love of Jesus to these precious little children.

Recently the sponsor of a child in one school wanted to personally meet her two "adopted" children. Each attended a Nazarene primary and secondary school. This sponsor had been sending her monthly support for several years. She had recently decided to sponsor a second child. The missionaries were asked to bring both children to the end of the road so the sponsor could meet them and attend church in the town nearby. As the greetings were exchanged, it was a life-changing experience for this Nazarene lady from "far-off" America. She had never worshiped with people of another culture and language. But what changed her life forever was the startling difference in the two children. The girl was bright and healthy, and fidgeted all through church. (Sound familiar?) But the little boy, who was there with his father, didn't move, didn't smile, and wasn't very alert. What made the difference? Five years of hot lunches in the Nazarene primary school. The little girl had been receiving these lunches since age three. She was happy, healthy, alert, and fun. The little boy, age eight, had only started school one month before. He will never be as big as a normal child; he probably will not do as well in school as the other children. He had protein deficiency during the first eight years of his life.

That Nazarene lady went back home a new person. She didn't need to read the quarterly updates on the school feeding program to understand that it works. She now knows why all the time, energy, and effort are given to these feeding programs. "Jesus loves you, and I do too."

Merely feeding people is not the ultimate solution. One answer is this: "If you want to feed a kid, give his dad a job." Not bad advice, *if* there is a job to give.

Another answer is summarized in a word most of us don't often use: *agmission.* Nazarene missionaries long ago learned it does little long-term good to provide relief feeding or safe water unless the recipients learn how to produce food for themselves and maintain their own water systems. Agmission trains specialized missionaries in critically important ministries. Mid-America Nazarene College offers the beginning step in this process: a four-year program with a major in agmission. This degree, coupled with a master in missiology from Nazarene Theological Seminary, is the academic route followed by an increasing number of young people who feel called into this special type of missionary service. Think of it! The lack of pure water is the biggest killer of children on this planet. Increased food production provides self-sufficiency. Without these agmission programs, we would be feeding for a long time with no hope of ever doing anything else.

In 1984, agmission projects comprised 7 percent of the overall ministry of NCM. They are the "other end" of many of the feeding programs being conducted. For example, in Mozambique, 1,000 hoes and thousands of pounds of seed were delivered to the refugees under the care of NCM by missionary Dennis Riggs and NCM associate Rodney Adkins. These hoes and seeds are the literal answer to the question "How long can we feed these people?" The answer is 12 months, at a cost of nearly $10,000 per month. At the end of 12 months these refugees, on land provided by the government, will be harvesting their own crops and drinking from their own water sources. Agmission is the answer to the physical problems of more millions of people than you could ever count. Can you imagine the effectiveness of agmissionaries developing these techniques with willing people who do not yet know Jesus?

One such professional agmissionary is Dr. Glenn T. Fell. He is working in Africa on a specialized assignment for the Church of the Nazarene to Ciskei. Dr. Fell is the senior head of the agriculture program of the Fort Cox College of Agriculture and Forestry. He is an expert in soil science.

Dr. Fell is in Africa to upgrade the farming techniques of the people and to train young people in agriculture. His influence is great. One meeting, described by Dr. Fell, represents the encounters by missionaries all around the developing world:

> The meeting started typically late. . . . I was asked, being a visitor and this being a meeting organized by a Christian rural development agency, to share from the Word of God. I shared some scripture and my testimony, mentioning how I felt God had led me to serve Him in Ciskei. When I finished, the village headman, as is customary, stood up to give his response to my words. He expressed his gratefulness for my visit and my interest in his people, but what remains clearly in my mind were his comments that the people would know I was sent from God if I could bring water to their village.

NCM is funding a water project for Dr. Fell. This is mission. This is where the people live, suffer, and flock to those who at least seem to offer answers to their everyday needs. Dr. Fell isn't a preacher, but he is preparing the soil for the gospel seed to be planted. The gospel can come in many different forms, not the least of which is pure water.

Another example of agmission projects are the grain mills being developed in Malawi. These projects are under the supervision of Rev. Don Messer. One grain mill is already fully operational. A second has also been funded and will soon be completed. These facilities provide a much-sought-after alternative to the grinding of corn by stone or pole. They increase the yield and provide added income to the Nazarene Malawi farmers, as well as many other farmers in the areas who are seeking such assistance.

All these projects add to the supply of food in areas where every ounce produced counts. A small increase in the yield can mean the difference between life and death for many people. The feeding programs funded by NCM will continue. As the requests are received and processed, container after container of food will continue to flow into areas of famine and drought. But long after the last ship has docked at the port of entry and the last truck has delivered the last sack of rice, maize, beans, or some other high-protein food blend to the people, they will be holding the hoes, axes, and other items that will help them help themselves. We agonize over those haunting eyes staring at us from the television screen. But we can sleep better this night, knowing that not only the food trucks are rolling, but the agmissionaries are there, in ever-increasing numbers, to deliver the love of Jesus in ways few of us had ever thought possible.

> "Christianity that does not begin with the individual does not begin. Christianity that ends with the individual ends."
>
> —E. Stanley Jones

6

Help Yourself

PORTUGAL

On April 25, 1974, the nation of Portugal experienced a convulsive change in government. There had been in place for decades a conservative dictatorship that was committed to its colonial holdings, particularly in Portuguese Africa. The two major countries in Portuguese Africa were Angola and Mozambique. Others include the Cape Verde Islands and Portuguese Guinea (now Guinea-Bissau).

As the nation passed through the unstable waters of change, long-suppressed voices were heard, and many underground political parties surfaced. The government that finally emerged was democratic in its orientation.

The political convulsion gave independence movements in the colonies the opportunity to seize power and remove the colonizers. From the colonies came two groups of people, the *refornados* (returnees) and the refugees.

The returners were those thousands of citizens born in Portugal—military, civil servants, businessmen, teachers, merchants, and traders—but who had lived and worked in the colonies. Suddenly the Portuguese homeland was inundated with returnees. Housing and jobs had to be found as they attempted to reintegrate into Portuguese society.

The second wave of arrivals were the refugees—thousands of Africans motivated by fear of the consequences of independence in the ex-colonies. Most brought their entire families. They were African by birth but Portuguese by culture. In this case, however, the refugees had no home and no roots to identify with. The economic problems of housing, education, health care, and employment have been enormous.

Many refugees had no marketable skill and minimal formal education. The poorest live in deplorable plastic or wooden shacks, with no sanitation, often invading dumpsters for food.

The Church of the Nazarene had long and well-established work in Mozambique and Cape Verde. In the influx came four trained pastors who immediately started contributing to the work. The Nazarene church was planted in Portugal just before the 1974 revolution. The arrival of these pastors, and many laymen, particularly from Cape Verde, has given unusual growth and stability to the church in Portugal.

With money provided by Nazarene Compassionate Ministries, the church has been able to help these refugees in three specific ways.

1. Distribution of fruit and blankets after a devastating flood that destroyed the camps in 1983.

2. In June 1985 the president of European Nazarene Bible College, Rev. Walter Crow, spent a week establishing and training in a self-help project making decoration marble balls out of rough, quarried rock. NCM money made possible the purchase of the equipment. An oversight committee supervised the project, and the church in Lisbon, as well as missionaries Sraders and Scotts, were deeply involved.

3. Rev. Crow also helped establish a second self-help project—a furniture reupholstery shop.

The self-help approach is self-supporting, provides training and income, and perhaps most of all gives a sense of worth and integrity to the individual.

ZAMBIA

As churches strive for self-support, income generation becomes critical. In Zambia, Africa, a unique experiment is in process. Adjustments are being made, and there are shortages of equipment. Nevertheless, the seed money from NCM has made possible yet another self-help project.

Zambia Lima—An Experiment in Self-support

Although necessity may not always be the mother of invention, it is often the mother of creative thinking. Such was the case with the Zambia Church of the Nazarene.

In 1981 it became clear to both Zambian and missionary leadership that the church subsidy program was a failure. Churches that had been on subsidy for many years were not moving toward self-support. It was decided that both the North and South districts would embark on a subsidy cutback program. Although at first faith was weak, the need was obvious and the break was made.

The subsidy cutback was designed to take place over a period of five years. There would be no negotiations; 20 percent each year would be cut back by the district and assumed by the local church. The pastors and local church committees agreed to give it a try.

In the second year of the subsidy cutback the Zambia Lima program was developed on an experimental basis on the North District. In the third year of the program, one new church was started on subsidy, five new churches were organized as self-supporting, and all the churches that had formerly been on subsidy went self-supporting. A similar pattern developed on the South District as well.

These rapid and exciting developments came about in large part because of the Lima program. A lima in Zambia stands for a small farming plot of one or two acres. Due to the dwindling supply of copper ore in the country the government has strongly been urging the development of the farming sector. The Church of the Nazarene saw the need and the opportunity to be involved in this development. In turn this became one of the primary motivating factors behind the Lima project.

A second, but equally important, motivation behind the project was the need to supplement pastors' salaries. If the district was no longer willing to subsidize the local church, and the local church was struggling to pay a pastor's salary, then the districts needed to provide an alternative source of income for the pastors. In this area the philosophy of mission was strongly influenced by Roland Allen in his book *The Spontaneous Expansion of the Church.*

Writing in 1927, Allen states, "Nothing is so weakening as the habit of depending upon others for those things which we ought to supply for ourselves. Nothing more undermines the spirit which should express itself in spontaneous activity. How can a man propagate a religion which he cannot support, and which he cannot expect those whom he addresses to be able to support?" (35). He goes on to write that the pastors with the most influence in their community are the pastors that are able to support themselves. Thus the Zambia Lima project was born.

Through a $5,000 grant from NCM, a Lima Loan Fund was started. This money would be available to pastors or churches that could meet the requirements set up in the loan agreement. These agreements were drawn up by District Superintendent Steve Doeer in consultation with the pastors who were going to be using the loan fund. They were designed to be simple yet complete. They are as follows:

1. Money is to be loaned for the development of farming plots and to provide access to the market. The lima must be close enough to the pastor so as to be closely supervised by him without conflicting with his pastoral duties.

2. The purpose of this loan program is to supplement the income of the pastor or congregation in order to alleviate the need for regular subsidies from the district. It is not meant to be a permanent, ongoing subsidy itself. It is expected that good principles of business management will be used in the development of limas. Therefore the loans will be available for a maximum of five years to any one pastor or congregation.

3. As much as possible the money will be given in the form of checks, and a receipt will be signed by the recipient of the money.

4. The maximum loan will be for the development of two hectares of land. The amount will be determined by the crop to be planted according to the government figures for current production costs.

5. It is expected that the total loan will be repaid at the end of the current growing season. If full repayment is not possible, a minimum of 50 percent of the initial loan must be repaid before financing would be considered for a second year. If refinancing is necessary, the new loan cannot exceed the total amount of the original loan.

Crops planted in November 1984 were harvested in June and July 1985. Although loan payments have not been collected yet, it is expected there will be a 60 percent repayment the first year. It has been a learning process for all involved. For most it is the first time they have tried to farm on this scale, and in some cases actual costs have exceeded expectations. Tractors for plowing and disking are almost non-existent. Transportation for supplies and marketing is difficult to arrange and is expensive. Weeding and harvesting is time-consuming and backbreaking.

But the benefits are already becoming obvious. The pastors have been able to lift their heads and know they are no longer dependent on, or subservient to, foreign funds. The church laity have learned to accept the new role of their pastors and for the most part have encouraged him to be bi-vocational. Both church and pastor are learning important lessons in financial responsibility that are assisting them in church administration. Finally, a spirit of new life and spontaneity has broken out on the district. New preaching points are being started regularly. Six new churches were organized in the first year. An air of expectation has sprung up as men and churches learn to trust God and follow the leading of His Holy Spirit into new adventures of faith.

These are brief examples to make the one point: Money can be invested to start a self-help project that will stretch its net effect for many years into the future. It is a good return on a small investment.

7

The Healing Touch

The veteran missionary escorted the young lady to "the hospital." Dr. Orpha Speicher, M.D., had recently arrived in Washim (Basim) after a long and wearing journey by ship from the United States.

Her training in medicine at Loma Linda University had been a lengthy process. Initially the only reason she entered medical school was to follow the instruction of General Superintendent H. F. Reynolds: "Young lady, if you want to become a missionary, become a medical doctor." Orpha's call was to become a missionary, although she thought as a teacher.

Now here she was—ready to view the building that was to become the Nazarene hospital in India. To her horror, she looked at a building that had been a school but was now closed. There were rats, birds, and bugs infesting the building. The rooms were stacked with broken furniture, the walls covered with black boards, the plaster falling and cracked.

She turned to the veteran. He smiled and said, "This is your hospital. You will have to create what you want." The young surgeon, out of the United States for the first time, in a new country with a difficult language, discovered there was no equipment, no trained staff, no nurses, no patients, no money—and in this unpretentious way, Reynolds Memorial

Hospital was born. Orpha Speicher did it all. She overcame suspicion and hostility in the town; cleaned, scrubbed, and repaired the building; lobbied for money; and began to train staff. Through the years she drove trucks, mixed cement, designed buildings, and started a nurses' training school.

Dr. Orpha Speicher typifies the commitment of those in compassionate ministry. No task is too large, no job too small, no assignment too dirty, no challenge too awesome, to undertake in the name of Christ.

The "Speicher story" has always been happening in missions and compassionate ministries. Dr. David Hynd carved out a hospital in Bremersdorp (now Manzini), Swaziland. Dr. T. Harold Jones did the same in Acornhoek, Republic of South Africa (the Ethel Lucas Memorial Hospital). In later years, Dr. Dudley Powers was founding medical superintendent in Papua New Guinea.

In pioneering work it has always been that way and always will be. Medical missions—health concern and care—has always been part of the Christian mandate. Name the most famous missionaries—Carey, Livingstone, Schweitzer, Moffat, Morrison, and so on—and all have had a medical component as part of their ministry. It might be an aspirin, a bandage, a salve for tropical sores, comfort during deadly epidemics, a stethoscope, even a Band-Aid—missions and medicine have gone together like a horse and carriage.

In this book we are not giving a history of nor philosophy of medical missions. We are telling a sampling of some things happening today in this phase of compassionate ministry.

Third World Medicine

The emphasis for medical missions in the third world should be on preventive rather than curative medicine. India is a case in point.

India is the world's second most populous nation: nearly

800 million. About 80 percent of India live in villages or rural areas, which are serviced by 20 percent of India's health care professionals. India is moving toward a health care delivery system that will assure basic health care for all its citizens by A.D. 2000.

One of every four babies born dies before age five. Of these deaths 46 percent die of diseases brought on by malnutrition. The cultural norm in India is for each family to produce enough children so that at least one son will grow to adulthood and be able to support the parents in their old age. Large families, often with too little food and certainly no extra money, cannot buy medicines for illness. Often, therefore, families must make the choice whether to let sick members die, thus saving enough to have food for the rest to eat, or to help cure sick members and put the remainder of the family at risk. It is a vicious circle.

Reynolds Memorial Hospital (the same founded by Orpha Speicher) offers a ray of hope in an essentially rural part of central India. The hospital is offering a "rural development program" to help people prevent disease that robs them of limited resources. In brief, here is how it works.

1. Catering to needs in rural areas as opposed to requiring all medical services to be performed in the hospital.
2. Developing a comprehensive program of
   a. disease prevention
   b. controlling size of family
   c. environmental hygiene
   d. purchase of food
   e. nutritional training
3. Conducting "Under Five" clinics. Every child under five is monitored for weight gain, assessed regularly for nutrition and food intake, immunized against childhood disease, while mothers are trained to space children two years apart and to value a small family.
4. A feeding program is sponsored in the hospital. There is

no central kitchen in the hospital because food taboos prohibit the use of animal proteins and *preparation of food by those who do not observe such practices.* Rather, the hospital distributes basic staples of Indian diet (wheat, jowari milo, lentils, spices, oil, onions, vegetables) to the families of sick patients so each family may feed their own.

Hunger and Disaster funds have been used to purchase these basic food staples. The food is cooked in an area set aside for patients' families over sulas (open woodstoves), while one member of each family stays with the patient.

Without this program many families would remove seriously ill patients from the hospital without the doctor's permission to save money. Thus, food distribution saves lives.

In third world health care, curative medicine (hospitals, doctors, Western technology) must give precedence to preventive medicine (volunteer trainers, nutritionists, clinics, simple remedies, community/public health). Note the following illustration:

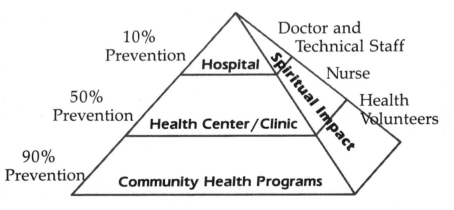

Third World Health Care

The above illustration indicated that in many third world settings many more people are contacted on a less sophisticated level medically. But when the contacts include the presence of dynamic and witnessing Christians, there can be a greater spiritual impact.

The Brazil Clinic

In December 1984 the following official invitation was received by the World Mission Division:

THE CHURCH OF THE NAZARENE
OF BRAZIL-RIO/SAO PAULO DISTRICT,

moved by the great love of Jesus, for the whole man—body, soul, and spirit—has the great honor of inviting you and your family to attend the dedication of its first "NAZARENE CLINIC" (future Nazarene Hospital), which ceremony will take place on December 28, 1984, as follows:

7:00 P.M.—Service of praise and gratitude in the Olinda Church of the Nazarene, located at Rua Manuel Reis, 931. The messenger for the occasion will be the district superintendent, Rev. J. A. Lima.

8:00 P.M.—The guests will proceed to the clinic on the same street, Rua Manuel Reis, 377—for the unveiling of the dedicatory plaque and to visit the premises.

For the Board of the Clinic

REV. JOAQUIM ANTONIO LIMA   DR. HAROLDO MILLET NEVES
President   *Vice-president*

The Rio-Sao Paulo District in the dynamic nation of Brazil was starting a medical ministry. In the words of Rev. Joaquim Lima, district superintendent, our "primary responsibility is to reach persons and souls with the full gospel of our Lord Jesus Christ. However, it also [is an] urgent need to involve . . . members to a greater extent in the community."

A Nazarene medical doctor, Dr. Haroldo M. Neves, had

challenged the district to establish a Nazarene medical clinic in a needy region of Baixada Fluminense, Rio de Janeiro. The district has accepted the challenge. Churches of the Nazarene in and around the 10 million population center of Rio have become partners in contributing to the support of the clinic. The District Advisory Board has accepted all legal and supervisory responsibility.

NCM has been able to assist with equipment funding for ultrasound equipment, electrocardiogram equipment, office and record keeping equipment, air conditioners and fans, a bed, linens, and other medical supplies—even a drinking fountain.

Now there is a viable medical outreach in Brazil in an impoverished area—a part of the compassionate outreach of the Brazilian church. Dr. Neves is not unlike the Speichers, Hynds, Joneses and others of an earlier generation, carving out a ministry of compassion in the name of Christ.

There should be no surprise. When Western-sponsored missions spurred the expansion of the Christian faith and message, they carried with them all the ingredients of compassion that *are the natural* by-product of that faith. Now, in an emerging era of third world missions, exactly the same process is being repeated.

When visitors from North America arrive, this new reality makes a profound impression. In 1985 five volunteer businessmen, members of Arizona Nazarene Lands, Inc., from the Arizona District, visited Brazil. Included on the itinerary was the newly opened clinic. As Dr. Neves showed the small building and explained the great need, these laymen began to realize that the missionary impulse to go, send, and do was not confined to the West, the North, or any other region of the world. It was quite simply part of Christian compassion and was to be sensed wherever the name of Christ is named, and believing disciples are obedient.

Guatemala Medical Missions

The Brazil clinic story is being duplicated in Guatemala, this time at the initiative of Dr. Carlos Helmar Juarez Moya. He is a Nazarene medical doctor and the social action director of the NYI Convention of the district of Verapaces in Guatemala.

In his initial proposal, Dr. Moya used the following reasoning to begin again medical work in the country.

PROJECT:

GENERAL CONSIDERATIONS:

The Church of the Nazarene has a missionary church par excellence that has always tried to address man as an integral being—with spiritual needs but also with material needs and problems.

In Guatemala, since the beginnings of the Nazarene work, the church extended itself to the community. The churches grew and beside them were established other ministries: Nazarene schools, printing presses, clinics, and so on.

With the district becoming regular and the withdrawal of the North American missionaries from the field, this community extension began to disappear until none was left.

A few years ago we began to see the needs of the church: the pastors who don't know what to do when confronted with the problems of the brethren, the illnesses of children and adults, and communities with no health facilities. Sickness brings with it another set of problems: work disability, poverty, and more sickness.

We have seen the need to have educators in the church, integral educators of Christian education, reinforced by other elements: literacy, health education, agricultural education, education for the home, and others.

Our church district has several capable and willing agents for service to the church, but our district does not have the financial resources to develop these programs. We have tried to provide some services, but these have been individual attempts with personal funds. The attempts end or are suspended when the funds run out.

For three years I have been in charge of directing the District Board of Christian Life and Sunday School. This has provided me with the opportunity of visiting the entire district, observing the needs of the brethren, and receiving requests to begin works among them.

One year ago, a permanent Committee for Social Action was formed within the NYI Convention. I presided and the requests of the brethren for us to attend to their situation were more intensely manifested.

The requests are specific: We want medical help and medicines for our illnesses.

When we have been able to get some medicine, we have made medical tours to zones far from the district, taking some relief to the needy.

Attempts have been made to install clinics in the churches of Salama, Tactic, and San Juan Chamelco. These have functioned and some continue to function, but with many limitations.

Construction is in progress on a clinic in the church of Saholomm, but we lack the financial resources for equipment and medicines.

Work has been going on in San Miguel Chicaj since February of 1984. A clinic has been built, and some equipment and medicine donations have been obtained. A kitchen was built and a program of nutrition has been established for the children. A literacy program was begun, and 75 brethren (adults) learned to read in 1984. Ten brethren learned first aid and how to attend to child delivery and minor health problems. These are helping in the church and the community. Lack of financial resources has greatly limited their efforts.

Our intention is to continue in this task, attending to the needy. We want to interest more individuals in this ministry, but financial resources limit us. We have no vehicle to mobilize ourselves throughout the district. We don't have a continuous supply of medicine. We don't have the teaching aids in the church: electricity, film projector, slide projector, and so on.

We believe that if we have these aids we can begin a strong evangelistic ministry and help the needy of our district. Their needs are many and great.

During the district assembly we received requests from all

the churches to give lay training courses on the various aspects of Christian education. Ten pastors asked us to hold monthly clinics in their churches. I have to recognize it is impossible for me to attend to everything, because of other obligations, but if I can give much, and if we count on equipment and transportation, we could interest others in participating in the task and find laymen who can develop an extension ministry in the church.

With grants now from Nazarene Compassionate Ministries, some of the needed equipment has been acquired. This involves the procurement and maintenance of basic medical equipment, but also equipment for evangelism such as an electric generator, slide projectors for visual presentations, and educational aids.

Three items in this new venture are of particular interest:

1. The motivation for compassionate ministry arises naturally from the Christian mandate to serve. This was not a ministry imposed from a foreign source, but one which comes from the indigenous national church.
2. Subsidy funding for such projects from Nazarene Compassionate Ministries do not drain the General Budget but come from other income sources.
3. This project is seen as a responsibility of a social action arm of the official youth organization—Nazarene Youth International. In reflection, this has many reminders of the quality of involvement which characterized the Church of the Nazarene in the early 20th century. NYI can officially engage in some highly significant social issues.

Medical missions in the name of Christ continues from one generation to another—one setting to another. Apparently the need will never end, and the response will always be present among Christ's faithful servants.

The Upper Amazon

Dr. Larry and Addie Garman have brought the work among the Aguaruna Indian peoples of the upper Amazon basin to a place of revival, church growth, and stability. Medicine has always been part of this work, but today it is moving to meet new challenges.

Funding through NCM has been made available to equip with medicine the Nazarene clinic so that the physician's assistants can administer these in isolated villages. These are areas so remote as to be nearly inaccessible to Peruvian commercial life. The greatest problem has been putting medicine into the hands of those trained to treat *at a local level.*

In effect, the effort is to develop a network of village clinics, each manned with a trained assistant, thus alleviating the crushing load at the main clinic and making health care more available. Interestingly, Nazarene pastors will be trained as the physician's assistants. This will give them credibility and increase the effectiveness of their spiritual ministry.

In addition, there will be a training of male nurses who can ply the two or three major rivers of the area (literally the streams of commerce). Again, these nurses will also be pastors. The training course will be three years in length and include both public health and Bible/ministerial studies. Those who already have medical training will be required to study evangelism and Bible. Those who are already pastors will be required to study public health.

There are many other medical programs in operation presently. In most of the developing nations, health care through preventative and curative medicine, and training for a better life, is of great significance. Christ understood this long ago when He mandated a healing ministry in the world.

8

No Place
to Call Home

Few of us can really understand the sobering thought: "I can never go home." There are many different definitions of what a refugee is or is not. Some of these definitions are political; others are economic. For the sake of this presentation, a refugee is anyone, for whatever reason, who can't go home.

Displaced persons are a different problem. Displaced people are just that: people who have been displaced by man-made or natural disaster. Even though the causes are quite different, the response is nearly always the same. People who have lost their place of residence, and are struggling to understand what has happened to them, what they should do next, and where to go have special needs. Most of us will never experience the totally disconcerting feeling of having no home, no base, no center, no turf, no stability, no special closet to store the things of our lives. We can barely understand even a small portion of the suffering, the terror, the need to belong, the need for help. As the politics of our world continue to destabilize and disturb, people are increasingly impacted. On every hand are people who have been displaced, refugees from war, famine, or some other tragedy. The way they live their lives, view God, and understand themselves has undergone traumatic change. To these people the Church of the Nazarene must continually be ready to minister. For these people must learn that God *does* love them. They learn that best when they see us love them.

NCM follows the following policy in regards to refugees and displaced persons.

1. If it is possible to voluntarily resettle these people back into their place of origin, we do all we can to make this possible. A good example of this process is the people who lost their homes in the Philippines due to the typhoons and volcanic eruptions. The Nazarene missionaries in charge of our response did all they could to assist these people to rebuild their homes in the very same locations they had lived in before these tragedies struck.

The same procedure was followed in Mexico City after the earthquake. The displaced people were assisted in the rebuilding of their lives as closely as possible to the way they were prior to the earthquake.

2. If voluntary resettlement back to the place of origin is not possible, then we assist in the resettlement of these people into an area of the same region from where they came and with people of their same cultural grouping. Examples of this is the assistance being offered to the Ethiopians in Sudan, and the Mozambicans in the Republic of South Africa. These people are refugees. As much as they might want to return to their respective homelands, it is not possible. NCM is assisting in their resettlement into areas where they can be with people who speak the same language and share the same cultural heritage.

One of the most exciting projects is in Central America. The church is actively involved in refugee work among children. Some Guatemalan children cannot go home because their homes have been destroyed or families killed. This story can be repeated in many areas of Central America and other parts of the world.

In Guatemala the Church of the Nazarene has established a children's home for these young people. Their stories are far too gruesome to share, but suffice it to say that children are victims of man's ability to torture and maim.

These children were all brought to the home by people in the surrounding area who found them wandering in the mountains, hiding for their very lives, and totally traumatized with fear. All have lost their families through torture, murder, rape, and other depraved acts. It is difficult to imagine how such things could be perpetrated against helpless, defenseless people.

But the church was there, ready, willing, and thankfully able to give the love of Jesus in action. The home was officially dedicated on January 17, 1985. Initially 50 orphaned children were at the center. Since there are thousands of such children in the area, the total number of orphans taken into the home will ultimately depend upon the amount of financing, support, and administrative personnel available.

The home is administered by a committee comprised of Guatemalan Nazarene church leaders, a member of the Central American Regional office staff, and one representative from the office of Nazarene Compassionate Ministries in Kansas City. The home receives no General Budget support and is entirely dependent upon donations for its survival.

One approach that has helped greatly to stabilize this ministry is a newly inaugurated one-to-one sponsorship program. Each of these orphans has been given a willing and loving Nazarene sponsor. These are "adoptive parents" who send monthly support. They pray for these children to grow to learn of Jesus and His love, in spite of the terrible things they have experienced.

Current cost of sponsorship is $30.00 per month per child. Additional costs are covered through donations made to the Nazarene Hunger and Disaster Fund.

There is no better way to express gratitude to the entire church for this ministry than to quote the president of Guatemala. In his letter to the Regional Office of the Church of the Nazarene, the president said:

"I extend my most sincere congratulations to you for your unselfish labor on behalf of the needy children, future citizens who need guidance on the path of good. Your efforts are worthy of recognition. Let me reiterate my high esteem and consideration for you."

These children are no longer afraid to sleep with the lights out. They are healthy, normal-looking children, learning to read and write, and growing up to be the citizens of Guatemala. But something else is happening to them. They are learning of the love of Jesus from Nazarene schoolteachers, social workers, and a local Guatemalan pastor who serves as administrator of the home.

There were so very many people who became involved in this ministry, it is hard to begin to list them. Mr. and Mrs. Dale Black, from Long Beach, Calif., should be thanked for all of their early efforts in seeing this children's home become a reality. Others include the Dr. Robert Hudson family, and Mr. Bob Prescott of the NCM staff in Kansas City. They have assisted in the building of buildings and securing of sponsors.

3. If resettlement of refugees into their own area of origin or culture is not possible, then resettlement into another area within the same world region is the third choice. In these cases, the cultural bridging and assimilation into the new host culture is much more difficult and requires time, money, and patience.

Examples of this type of program can be found once again in Central America. In these troubled nations, such as

El Salvador and Nicaragua, people have fled from their home countries looking for safety and a chance to start a new life.

Their stories are no less heart-wrenching than those of the little children of Guatemala. In most of these situations NCM is working in combination with other relief agencies such as the C.E.S.A.D. in El Salvador. In these responses, the Nazarene funding is used to help relocate these people into neighboring countries. Many missionaries are hard at work assisting in their physical well-being and giving to them the story of eternal life that comes only from Jesus.

The last chapter on these situations has not yet been written. Will NCM need to establish additional children's homes for defenseless orphans? Only time will tell. But as the national churches of this region seek to minister, it should be every Nazarene's duty from around the world to pray earnestly for fellow Christians working in these areas.

4. When all the above options prove impossible, a fourth and last option is available: resettlement into another country which is far removed from the refugee's home culture and language. An example of this type of resettlement is the many Cambodians, Laotians, and Vietnamese who are resetting into the United States. Many of these have known nothing but war and suffering for an entire generation. Another group is the northern Ethiopians who have fled their home country in the face of certain death for their beliefs and/or tribal backgrounds.

Here is the mission field coming to us. Here is a chance for the Church of the Nazarene to minister to people from countries where there is no Church of the Nazarene. These people, many of whom are finding Christ as their Savior, are now preparing to return to their home country to present the gospel to their fellow countrymen. The same is true of the Ethiopians in this country. NCM is working to assist in their ministry of relief and love to their countrymen.

Here is "mission by personal involvement" for literally any Church of the Nazarene anywhere. NCM is working closely with World Relief in the placement of these "class four" refugees into the United States. The transition is enormously difficult. They need to learn English. They need to become employable in another culture. God forgive us if we miss this opportunity from God to do mission in our own backyard. Many Nazarene churches are engaging in ethnic ministries. Many more need to do likewise. Haitians are in Wisconsin, picking onions; Southeast Asians are in Central Ohio, attempting to learn English; and Cambodians are in Long Beach, Calif., striving to build a dynamic church. Hardly any region in the Western world is unaffected by this mass migration of needy peoples. These needy people are marching literally by our church doorsteps in search of someone to tell them the meaning of life.

People who cannot go home face many problems. On the other hand, if the church responds with compassion, the homeless can make an earthly home as they prepare for an eternal home.

"We are experiencing a rebirth of social concern and compassion as an authentic expression of holiness."
—William T. Greathouse

9

No Exemptions Here!

THE HERITAGE

As we observed in chapter 2, Nazarene compassionate ministry in the United States is nothing new. In the early years of the Church of the Nazarene it was a very visible and active part of ministry. Later it was less visible—secondary to other priorities and needs, but yet never absent.

It is important to remember that most compassionate ministry occurs in the local church. It is a body of believers visiting the sick, feeding the hungry, touching with love a specific need. Thus, compassionate ministries rises out of a theology of love, concern, and active caring. Indeed it is a natural and normal outgrowth of what is in the heart—the essence of the human spirit empowered by God's Spirit.

In a survey of the Church Extension Ministries office nearly half of all local Nazarene churches in the United States described specific ministries of their church that could be described as "compassionate."

The many changes in American society since 1960 have brought the local church unusual challenges (some would say stresses). These changes include:

1. The greatest wave of immigrants since the early

1900s—only this time from Latin, Caribbean, and Asian regions.

2. Enormous changes in urban areas caused by civil rights, equal housing and employment opportunities, and court decisions. The urban migration has left many churches in cities the option of adapting, moving, or dying.

3. Local churches are reassuming responsibility in many areas because of the failure of government to provide required services.

4. Political and economic turmoil in many world regions, which has flooded the nation with undocumented "illegals" or those seeking sanctuary through church agencies.

This listing is by no means comprehensive but will briefly indicate the types of challenges local churches face.

SOME PROJECTS ALREADY KNOWN

The Manhattan Church of the Nazarene, also known as "the Lamb's," has been operating over 10 years very successfully in the Times Square area of Manhattan. Real estate (the Lamb's Club) purchased for $475,000 has escalated to $8 to $10 million in value.

The Lamb's has continually operated feeding programs, street ministries, counseling for drug dependency, and provided emergency housing. Now a hospice center is being considered, as well as many other programs. (See *Renew the Ruined Cities,* by Cook and Nees.)

The New Milford church, near New York City, has had a dynamic history of compassionate ministries along with explosive evangelistic growth. Pastor Charlie Rizzo, a product of the streets, can minister to people of the urban climate. (See the *New Milford Story,* by Cook and Truesdale.)

The New Bedford International Church, pastored for over 30 years by Rev. Manuel Chavier, has reached all levels of this community in New England. The church, originally Cape Verdian in character and with a special ministry to the Portuguese-speaking fishing community, has cut across all homogeneous lines to reach people of all races at their point of need.

Rev. Gilbert Leigh started New World Ministries many years ago while he pastored Ingleside Nazarene in southside Chicago. This independent agency, an outgrowth of a pastor's compassionate heart, has provided social/spiritual service to thousands through day-care, halfway houses, G.E.D. training, job counseling, Head Start programs, drug and alcohol counseling, and housing. The city of Chicago has conferred many honors on New World and its founding director.

Many churches, particularly in the Southwest, have been involved in migrant ministries. Thousands of workers, with their families, move with the harvests from place to place, often in inadequate housing and with little church contact.

It is important to note that any church hoping to minister effectively in urban areas must have a compassionate ministry component. It cannot be at arm's length or by proxy. It is at the doorstep of the church every minute of every day. Such overwhelming need places unusual stress on pastors and ministers and their families.

NEWER PROJECTS LESS KNOWN

This chapter will illustrate some projects being founded by Nazarene Compassionate Ministries in the United States. Note: This listing is only a sampling.

Disaster Relief

It was a late spring tornado. It swept out of Ohio, and as

80

cold and hot air clashed, the tornadic activity moved relentlessly and without regard across northwestern Pennsylvania. The Albion area was particularly hard hit—houses and businesses destroyed. People who lost everything—houses, clothing, furniture, even jobs—turned to the churches for help.

Pastor Donald Hennen, as part of an interfaith disaster recovery council, turned to NCM for help. And help was forthcoming to assist in this disaster from the Hunger and Disaster Fund.

A fire—the work of an arsonist—swept through a 24-hour child-care home for boys ages 13 to 21. The boys—all from broken homes, many orphaned, and most victims of child abuse—lost everything. The home lost furniture, clothing, and essential linens.

This home (Long Stretch Youth Homes) in Frostburg, Md., appealed for help. A member of the board, a longtime Nazarene and contributor to General Budget, had seen an article about hunger in Africa. She wondered, Would there be any help available? There was, through Hunger and Disaster funds.

Los Angeles First well illustrates the potential and problems encountered by an urban church. The average Sunday morning combined attendance of the church's five congregations is over 600.

The problem is that two-thirds of these are recent immigrants to the United States, and 80 percent live in the urban center of Los Angeles, with many of those classified as urban poor.

The cost of housing is high—a bare one-bedroom apartment runs $450 a month; minimum auto insurance starts at $1,000 per year.

Pastor Ron Benefiel and associate Fletcher Tink wondered, Could the church help? The primary needs they had were literally survival needs. Some members of the church were without housing or faced the threat of imminent eviction resulting from financial crises. Utilities were often turned off for lack of payment. Basic medical attention was unavailable.

The church has helped through NCM. Other ministries are being assisted also, such as crime and accident rehabilitation, counseling in family crises, and many other ministries. The goal of all this is to stabilize crisis/emergency/disaster situations so the church can open doors for evangelistic impact.

Feeding Programs

Hunger in America is a topic that always stirs hot debate. Is there hunger? How can there be hunger in a nation whose bins overflow with abundant crops?

Those on the front line of need spend little time debating the hunger issue. They are too busy responding to needs all around. The church through NCM has been helping.

The Central Florida District has tried to feed 900 migrant families, primarily Haitian, who got caught in the freeze fallout. Many of these families were already Christian and many Nazarene, including six who pastored Nazarene churches in Haiti but have relocated to Florida. NCM has helped restock depleted food shelves.

The Central Ohio District has become involved in a variety of ethnic ministries, including work among many Cambodian immigrants. As is true with most new arrivals, these refugees have many needs, including basic food staples. With the help of NCM, the district is meeting these needs.

The Haight-Ashbury area of San Francisco has evolved through many eras, including the hippie culture of the 1950s and 1960s. Today the Golden Gate Church of the Nazarene is attempting to minister to San Francisco in a comprehensive way.

One of these ministries is the Haight-Ashbury food program which is feeding over 200 people a day. Pastors Michael

Christensen and Michael Dotson noted funds running low. The program seemed essential, not only as an expression of Matthew 25, but to feed people with a wide variety of pathologies. It is important to keep these people working for themselves.

Would the church help? Yes, Hunger and Disaster funds would make it possible to keep the program alive and functioning.

Health Services

In many local churches varieties of health services are being provided. As noted earlier in this book, at one time a full hospital and nursing program was available in Idaho.

Today the most sophisticated health service being offered under direct auspices of the Church of the Nazarene in the United States is at the Community of Hope (COH), founded in inner-city Washington, D.C., by Dr. Tom Nees.

The Community of Hope Health Service is directed by Mrs. Lois Smith, R.N., M.N. About 5,000 to 6,000 medical care visits are being made in a calendar year by COH. In general the work is broken down as follows:

1. Pediatrics—About 25 percent of the patients are under 12 years of age. Three pediatric doctors and one pediatric nurse practitioner have volunteered time in this specialty. Many preventative services are provided in high-risk inner-urban Washington, D.C. Child abuse and infant mortality are often dealt with.

2. Adult services—Since about 25 percent of all Black adults suffer from high blood pressure, a Hypertension Management Clinic has been established. This clinic treats, trains, and provides medication free of charge to those who cannot pay, and encourages life-style change (drug abuse, exercise, nutrition, and diet). A part-time social worker assists with housing,

benefits, food, emergency funds, and other concerns.

Counseling services are offered, often spiritual in nature, to clients. A volunteer psychiatrist and family therapist assist.

There has developed a community outreach program with an advisory council of 10 "patients" who keep COH Health Services aware of changing community needs.

2. Adolescent Development and Health program. About 25 percent of patients are from 13 to 24 years of age. General health care is offered as well as counseling in specific teen needs—drug use, sexuality, social relationships, family responsibility, marriage, vocational aspirations, and dreams for the future. Family planning, including problems of unwanted pregnancies, are an important part of the service.

The church, through NCM, has made a grant to provide continuing support to the continuation and possible expansion of many of these programs.

Self-Help

Self-help is a simple concept: You help others to help themselves. It can take on some interesting and complex forms.

The Nazarene Indian Bible College (NIBC) is located a few miles south of Albuquerque, N.Mex., on 17 acres of land. President Denny Owens discovered that 8 of those acres was land suited for agricultural development. The land was flat and fertile and had available water.

Soon a decision was made to turn the land into income generation. Sheep and goats could be raised. Row crops and nursery stock could be grown for retail sale in the city. Students would do the work and generate income for both themselves and the college. NCM has allocated money for fencing, a cultivator, and a plow—self-help money.

84

Student income generation at NIBC is not unlike the agriculture programs. Shops are being set up on campus for auto mechanics, welding, plumbing, and upholstery work. The ceramic and pottery shop, already in operation, could be expanded.

This has several purposes. It provides income. It teaches students a marketable vocational skill, which may be used directly in church work or in a bivocational pastorate. Income goes to pay tuition and support the expense of the college.

Another NIBC project is a thrift store which warehouses clothing, furniture, and other items. Again, employment is offered, income generated, and a service provided for the community. NCM has provided start-up monies for these projects on the theory that each supports fully the mission of the college and the general evangelistic task of the church.

Another interesting example of self-help comes from a local Nazarene church, the Los Altos church, in Albuquerque, pastored by Robert Appleby. Long interested in city work, Appleby has engaged in some ambitious projects as an outreach of the church.

Recently a trailer court a few blocks from church was purchased. There are seven homes, including one Indian family, one Mexican refugee family, one invalid senior citizen, and four Cambodian families. The church is attempting to provide the low-income housing and cover the mortgage payments with outside money and rents.

A thrift store has been operated out of the church building. Recently NCM made a small grant to enable relocation of the store to an area that will generate more income (which, in turn, helps the shortfall on the trailer court). District Superintendent Leon F. Wyss says, "This is one of the finest inner-city, cross-cultural works that we have going anywhere in our denomination."

Yet another thrift store has been set up in Polk County, Florida. District Superintendent J. V. Morsch and coordinator

Nathan Price envision this as a key component of the huge impact being made among Haitian refugees. The store sells clothing at retail. Resale merchandise is solicited through community organizations by radio, TV, and newspaper solicitation. NCM provided funds to assist in initial lease of store space.

The spiritual impact of such compassionate ministry is significant. In the case of the Polk county store, impact is felt on the Lakeland (Fla.) Haitian Church of the Nazarene and the Haitian pioneer area. Opportunities for witness abound.

New Arrivals

Many projects involve new arrivals in the United States. A wave of immigrants brings a set of new challenges. These include job training and teaching English as a second language (ESL).

Long Beach First Nazarene and Senior Pastor John Calhoun have a dynamic and growing Cambodian ministry. Over 500 are now part of this outreach. Randy and Lorie Beckum pastor and head this work.

NCM has received a request to fund a cultural orientation and language tutoring center for Cambodians in Long Beach. ESL is taught by qualified teachers. A language lab with tape playback machines is being set up. This gives refugees an introduction to English and the Bible, since the Bible is an integral part of the ESL curriculum.

The same kind of project is being done in other places, such as Central Florida, where funds for books, materials, tables and chairs, and teachers have been granted.

Language learning is part of job training. Long Beach calls their effort a "resettlement care" program. Central Florida titles it "job counseling service." Many things are included: legal documentation, visits to Social Security and other offices, assessment of existing skills and training for new skills, and actual job placement. Randy Beckum states their threefold purpose:

1. Winning them to Christ and the church
2. Supplying basic needs and orientation to America
3. Dealing with the "second migration" of Cambodians who move to Long Beach from other parts of the United States

Staff members trained in evangelism give out Bibles to new arrivals and deal in areas of personal evangelism.

Nathan Price states, "As the new arrivals are employed, life becomes more orderly. They begin to develop a sense of accomplishment and self-worth as they are able to provide for themselves."

One side note: A one-hour radio program has begun in Creole and French in Florida. It announces help for new arrivals in immigration, job resources and training, health information such as where to go for care, and nutrition information. Interspersed is Christian music and announcements of Haitian church services. No wonder! The announcer is a Haitian Nazarene preacher!

Residential Programs

Some churches have established or plan to start residential programs. These would be centers that offer some housing and a myriad of ministry programming.

The Golden Gate Church in San Francisco presently operates a Men's Ministry Residential Program at the Oak Street house. Mr. Terry Workman is the current director. In this case the program design is men from the streets, that is, substance abusers and displaced persons. The program offers food, clothing, medical aid, and educational opportunities. Four men are admitted at a time, and the average stay is three to six months. Already 12 men have been enabled to establish a foundation of spiritual, emotional, and economic stability. NCM recently granted matching funds to assist.

In Chicago, which in 1986 is a special denominational target for spiritual impact, three centers are envisioned. These centers could include warehouses, apartment buildings, vacant supermarkets, and so on. Work and Witness teams could assist in renovation. Each center would provide:

1. Temporary emergency shelter care
2. Counseling programs
3. Job retraining
4. Referral services
5. Extension classes, including ESL

The centers would provide resources for existing Nazarene churches in the Chicago inner-urban area plus the new churches being planned. Hopefully this strategy will make a more efficient utilization of buildings and assets for all the churches. The church, through NCM, is committed to a major investment in the acquisition and start-up costs of these centers.

WRAP-UP

Again the authors need to underline two points:

1. What has been described above is a sampling, by no means complete. Many projects have not been mentioned.

   Also, things are developing so rapidly that the listing needs a daily, perhaps hourly, update.

2. This catalog of activity is done in the name of Christ. Note the history of compassionate ministry and its relationship to a theology of holiness (wholeness, the whole person, holism). All this activity is done for Christ and "unto the least of these." It is the spiritual impulse that fills, drives, and surrounds every action.

"The only gospel men see is the gospel according to you and me."
—George Hoffman

"In a nation whose bestseller list almost always includes one book on how to lose weight, we carry an unusual responsibility toward brokenness."
—Richard Schubert

10

Not by Proxy —Now Do It!

There are two ways to approach your involvement in mission. One way is "mission by proxy." This means we stay where we are, work where we work, and send others into the job of mission. Of course this is necessary. We certainly can't all drop everything we are doing and go off into full-time mission service.

Mission by proxy is accomplished through the sacrificial commitments of hundreds of Nazarene missionaries and specialized assignment personnel. In addition, there are thousands of national workers who are the backbone of any mission effort. These dedicated people are the "proxies" we send in our place when we pay our General Budget and special offerings. They also are the bulk of the delivery system in place whenever NCM moves into an area to meet needs. These people, whether they serve on a world mission region or in some type of urban, ethnic, or specialized ministry in their own country of origin, deserve not only our complete financial support but also our intercessory prayers. They need God's watchful care, protection, and special strength to carry out the great task of fulfilling the Great Commission.

Mission by proxy alone does not work. The vast majority of the world still does not know Jesus Christ as Savior. In excess of 1 billion people have never even heard who Jesus is, or as yet had a single opportunity to receive Him into their hearts. Another billion or so have only heard of Jesus through the mouth of a Marxist or follower of Islam. Can you imagine how a person who doesn't believe in Christianity explains who Jesus is? To express this another way, over one-half of the world has never yet had any real opportunity to accept the gospel message. They are waiting for someone to tell them.

The only way all of these millions of people will ever be confronted with Jesus is by an ever-growing cadre of volunteers who will help to supplement the dedicated professional missionaries and specialized assignment personnel. These volunteers are experiencing "mission by personal involvement." They are not only supporting mission by giving and praying, but more and more are giving of themselves to see the kingdom of God spread into new areas.

How does mission by personal involvement affect NCM? In the first place, it is affected through additional giving beyond the General Budget dollars. NCM is not a part of General Budget. Yet the General Budget makes possible the delivery system for NCM through missionaries and national workers who are already in place. This makes NCM the most cost-effective delivery system that can be found in any organization anywhere.

Another mission by personal involvement is the sponsorship program. Not only does this allow the donor to give to a specific area of need, but it ties the sponsor directly to the school that is being helped. The cost is currently $5.00 per month, and the money is used entirely for feeding schoolchildren in Nazarene elementary schools (the hot lunch program). The sponsor receives occasional updates on the school. Both the Nazarene Hunger and Disaster Fund and these project sponsorship programs are approved for 10 percent giving.

NCM has one-to-one sponsorships available to individuals, Sunday School classes, NWMS groups, who would like to become directly involved with one individual child. Pictures, letters, and information are exchanged on a regular basis. Because of the direct involvement of Nazarene missionaries and national workers, administrative costs are kept to a minimum, but 20 percent of all direct sponsorship monies are needed to pay these costs. This is not a 10 percent approved special project, but it does provide a means through which we can directly help needy children who are the responsibility of the Church of the Nazarene. Information on all these programs can be obtained by writing to the office of NCM and asking for sponsorship information.

Mission by personal involvement often means more than financial sacrifice. Some are able to leave home and business to experience mission in person. Nowhere has this type of involvement been more clearly articulated than the Nazarene Work and Witness program. Over 8,000 people in the last five years have been part of brief-term Work and Witness trips. What better way to become involved than by actually going and doing?

NCM currently has an ever-growing number of volunteer "associates" who are early retirees or who have taken a year away from their vocation to serve as full-time volunteer associates in doing compassionate ministries. One can only wonder how many more such Nazarenes there are, waiting for the opportunity to become involved.

Many of these volunteers wish to serve in supporting roles to current missionary and national staff. This program is called Nazarenes In Volunteer Service (NIVS). The participants are all self-funded volunteers who have skills they are using to assist the Nazarene missionary efforts worldwide. Medical doctors and other health professionals who go for a 3-month to 12-month period relieve missionary health professional staff for furloughs and continuing education courses. Other skills are in the areas of building trades, teaching, administration, computers, and agriculture.

These volunteers are the unsung heroes of missions. They serve without pay and provide most of their financing. Most are early retirees, a few are on sabbatical, and some are young people who have graduated from college and are eager to "give a year."

In addition to these individual volunteers is a growing group of volunteer organizations that serve as missionary support agencies. These groups represent a pooling together of Nazarenes with similar interests and/or vocational skills. One such group is the Nazarene Medical/Dental Fellowship (NMDF). This group is composed of doctors from various health fields who offer their services to NCM in times of emergency. They procure medicines, fill in for missionary doctors, or form Compassionate Ministry Work and Witness teams.

There are many other groups in various stages of formation. The Association of Nazarene Building Professionals has long been a key in the construction projects. More recently, the Nazarene Agmission Volunteers have formed a volunteer group to assist NCM in various agmission projects and the training of agmission personnel. Nazarene nurses have recently formed a similar organization.

The potential of volunteer activity in support of missions is staggering. Countries that are closed to traditional preaching ministries can be reached through volunteer and "tentmaking" missionaries. (These are people with skills who seek employment in countries where traditional missionaries are not allowed to enter.) They live and work and make contacts in these countries. They are a beachhead for later official entry. The blending of compassionate ministries and proclamation evangelism becomes another way to reach countless millions who have never heard.

NCM would like to suggest many activities that can be accomplished without disturbing the current living and working arrangements of individuals and families. For example, how much do you really know about hunger in our world? Have you ever considered becoming involved in learning enough about the issues that make a real difference in your world? It can be done. Your family, your youth group, your NWMS could become involved in some type of a "planned famine" or "hunger walk," with the money received going to help combat hunger in your local community and around the world through the Nazarene Hunger and Disaster Fund.

Some Nazarenes are becoming concerned about a lifestyle that has crept up on them. How much is enough? How much can we really spend on ourselves when so many are in desperate need? Hard questions, with no simple answers. Some are opting for simpler life-styles, and converting excess income to helping minister to those in need. Others are actively seeking to raise the level of awareness in local churches. Our people need to be reminded they have been blessed materially, and we all have a responsibility to minister to the poor of our world.

Something may have triggered a need in you to do mission by personal involvement. Write to the office of Nazarene Compassionate Ministries. Ask for information. Our world is hurting and needs to know about the love of Jesus. We all need to put that love into concrete, visible reality for those in need. Mission by personal involvement could become a lifestyle for thousands who are ready for the challenge of a lifetime.

Addendum on Education

Education has been an integral part of missions from the beginning. In fact, Jesus included the concept of teaching as part of His Great Commission to the disciples.

Through the centuries Christians have founded and staffed schools. This has been historically true throughout Europe and North America. Most of the distinguished Ivy League schools were originally sponsored by denominations, and many flatly stated in their statement of purpose that they existed to train ministers and missionaries.

In the Nazarene context, Dr. J. P. Widney, early associate of Dr. P. F. Bresee and a prominent physician in southern California, was president of the University of Southern California (USC), which was a Methodist-sponsored school.

The Church of the Nazarene has always sponsored many schools. In the early years the grandiose title of "university" was often used. Eventually these were consolidated into the present network of liberal arts colleges, graduate seminary, and Bible college.

Naturally, early missionaries took with them a concept of founding schools. Many of these were to train pastors or Bible women, and from them emerge today's outstanding network of ministerial training institutions. A discussion of these is beyond the scope of this book.

Other schools were secular in nature, offering a wide range of curriculum. These were begun in areas where the government was unable or unwilling to assume responsibility for educating children. They were primarily funded by the West and staffed by expatriates.

In Africa many of the present leaders are products of the mission school. In India, Alexander Duff in the 19th century established a concept of higher education that still influences the nation. Also in India the Nazarene Coeducational Christian School (NCCS) provided a model for a newly independent nation in integrating boys and girls into the same classes.

In other places, such as Haiti, Nazarene schools have provided early training through local churches to equip children to enter government-sponsored public schools. In many areas literacy training has been provided through the Laubach or other methods.

In Japan the church still sponsors a Japan Christian Junior College, which offers an English, business, and religion curriculum.

The point is, Nazarene missions has attempted to respond to need where need existed. This, along with medical missions, has been the two sides of historic and traditional compassionate ministries.

However, in recent years, secular Christian education has undergone dramatic transformation. As new governments have assumed control and responsibility, the need has changed, and many schools have been closed. Expatriates are now rarely used on the elementary level as missionary teachers except in schools designed and run for expatriate children.

Because of this changed scene in education, we have chosen not to include education as one of the chapters of current compassionate ministry.

There is one notable exception, however. Because of the unique relationship between the Church of the Nazarene and the government of Swaziland, the church sustains a dynamic and active educational ministry across that nation.

Mr. William Moon currently administers the program. It

consists of a high school, a teacher's training college, 35 elementary schools, and other interests. It is staffed by 20 expatriates and 380 contracted national teachers. Funding comes from government, church, and private sources.

One can safely assume that this educational ministry is continuing to have a major impact on the life of the nation and the growth of the church.

We salute those who through the years have poured their lives into young minds, carrying with them both human knowledge and the love of God, in the name of Christ.

Appendix

A listing of compassionate institutions, official or unofficial, listed in church documents, once sponsored by the church in North America.

Rescue Homes

1. Chicago—Rest Cottage, Rescue Home
2. Texarkana, Tex.—Rescue Home
3. Cincinnati—Hope Cottage
4. New York—Rescue Home, Brooklyn Rescue Home
5. Asheville, N.C.—Faith Cottage
6. Greensboro, N.C.—Rest Cottage No. 3
7. Columbus, Ohio—Rescue Home
8. Little Rock, Ark.—Door of Hope Mission
9. Oklahoma City—Rescue Home
10. Pilot Point, Tex.—Rest Cottage
11. Denver—Rescue Home
12. Arlington, Tex.—Berachah Industrial Home
13. South McAlester, Okla.—Berachah Rescue Home
14. Bowie, Tex.—Rescue Home
15. Providence, R.I.—Rest Cottage
16. Lynn, Mass.—Florence Crittenden Hope Cottage
17. Bethany, Okla.—Rescue Home, Nazarene
18. Hutchinson, Kans.—Refuge Home
19. Wichita, Kans.—Rescue Home
20. Oakland—Rescue Home
21. Kansas City—Rescue Home
22. Nashville—Door of Hope Mission, Pentecostal Training Home for Girls
23. Washington, D.C.—Rescue Home
24. Lake Charles, La.—Southwestern Training Home
25. Fort Worth—Bethel Mission
26. Old Fort, S.C.—Rescue Home
27. Davenport, Okla.—Rescue Home
28. Memphis—Beulah Training Home, Bethany Training Home

29. Snampscott, Mass.—Hope Cottage
30. Portland, Oreg.—Louise Home
31. Seattle—Lebanon Home
32. Elkhart, Ind.—Rescue Home

Children's Homes

1. Oklahoma City
2. Nashville
3. Pilot Point, Tex.
4. Peniel, Tex.
5. Bowie, Tex.
6. Eugene, Oreg.

Rescue Missions

1. Chicago—Apostolic Mission
2. New York—Water Street Mission, Cremorne Mission, Brooklyn Mission
3. Abilene, Tex.—City Mission
4. Dallas—Shelter
5. Providence, R.I.—People's Mission
6. Spokane, Wash.—Mission
7. Los Angeles—Fifth Street Mission
8. Lynn, Mass.—Mission
9. Washington, D.C.—Mission
10. Minneapolis—Mission
11. Little Rock, Ark.—Mission
12. Calgary, Alta.—Mission
13. Shreveport, La.—Mission
14. Fort Worth—Mission
15. San Antonio—Mission

Other

1. Indian Territory—Bethel Mission, Oklahoma Nazarene Indian Mission, South McAlester Mission
2. Winter City Missions—Many
3. Waco, Tex.—Prison Mission and Home for the Friendless
4. San Diego—The Rest (may have been retirement home)
5. Nampa, Idaho—Nazarene Missionary Sanitarium and Institute
6. Bresee—Chinese and Japanese missions, San Francisco Earthquake refugee relief

100

Glossary of Terms

Expatriate—One who lives and works in a foreign country. This typically includes such people as missionaries, diplomats, development specialists, and so on.

Third world—A grouping of lesser developed nations

Compassion—Suffering with the distress of others; displaying a strong motive to minister

Refugee—Someone who can never go home

Volunteer—Someone who has offered service to the church, most often without salary

Agmissions—Merger of the technology of agriculture with the motivation of missions

NCM—Nazarene Compassionate Ministries

ESL—English as a Second Language

Self-help—Helping others to help themselves

Delivery system—How to get what is needed to where it is needed

Bibliography

PRIMARY:

Benson, John T., Jr. *History of the Pentecostal Mission, Inc.,* 1898-1915.

Jernigan, C. B. *Pioneer Days of the Holiness Movement in the Southwest.*

Rees, Seth Cook. *Miracles in the Slums.* 1905.

Rest Cottage Association. *The White Slaves of America.* 1907.

Various District Assembly Journals—1909-12, 1919-20.

General Assembly Reports—Second to Fifth.

Various issues of *Herald of Holiness, Pentecostal Advocate, Purity Journal, Rest Cottage Messenger.*

Free Tract Society. *A Tragic End.* 1913.

Nazarene Missionary Sanitarium and Institute, Nampa, Idaho—Information Leaflet.

SECONDARY:

The Berachah Mission Periodicals, 1904-6, 1915-40.

Blaise, Leon E. "The Orphanage Question in the Church of the Nazarene." Paper submitted for seminar on studies in Nazarene history at Nazarene Theological Seminary, May 20, 1982. Deposited in Nazarene Archives, No. 192-34.

Herald of Holiness. "Unto the Poor the Gospel Is Preached," Diamond Anniversary Issue.

Manion, Lynn, and Jan Dolph. "A Short History of the Berachah Home and Berachah Cemetery." Paper submitted for City and Regional Seminar, University of Texas, Arlington, December 1979. From a copy deposited in Nazarene Archives, No. 192-34.

Nees, Tom. "The Holiness Social Ethic and Nazarene Urban Ministry." D.Min. project, Wesley Theological Seminary, 1976.

Parker, J. Fred. "Those Early Nazarenes Cared," *Preacher's Magazine,* fall, 1983.

Smith, Harold Ivan. *The Quotable Bresee.* Kansas City: Beacon Hill Press of Kansas City, 1983.

Smith, Timothy L. "Holiness Social Work in America, 1850-1910." Paper presented to the Nazarene Theological Seminary Breakfast Club, January 4, 1956. Deposited in Nazarene Archives, No. 727-14.

Tew, Vernon. "History of the Kansas City Rest Cottage." Paper submitted for seminar on studies in Nazarene history at Nazarene Theological Seminary, May 15, 1985. Deposited in Nazarene Archives, No. 790-4.

Further information on
volunteering, sponsorships, or other data
can be obtained from:

The Office of Nazarene Compassionate Ministries
World Mission Division
6401 The Paseo
Kansas City, MO 64131